JEAN MICHEL BASQUIAT

JEAN MICHEL BASQUIAT

Gemälde und Arbeiten auf Papier
Paintings and works on paper

The Mugrabi Collection

Herausgegeben von
Jacob Baal-Teshuva

Mit Beiträgen von
Jacob Baal-Teshuva,
Francesco Clemente, Jeffrey Deitch,
Henry Geldzahler, Jeffrey Hoffeld, A.R. Penck,
Richard Rodriguez

Museum Würth / Swiridoff Verlag

Dieser Katalog erscheint anläßlich der Ausstellung
im Museum Würth vom
27. September 2001 bis 1. Januar 2002

Die Ausstellung und der Katalog wurden durch
die großzügige und freundliche Unterstützung der
 Adolf Würth GmbH & Co. KG ermöglicht.

Realisation der Ausstellung: C. Sylvia Weber,
Beate Elsen-Schwedler, Kirsten Fiege, Sonja Klee,
Lun Tuchnowski

Sekretariat: Conny Ayen, Dorothea Truckenmüller

Übersetzungen: Philipp Mattson und
Carla Bassermann (Einführung C. Sylvia Weber)

Lektorat: Andrea Christa Fürst

Texterfassung: Theresa Mattson

Ausstellungstechnik: Michael Götzelmann, Ursula Kensy,
Gregor Kress, Ralf Maurer, Klaus-Martin Treder unter der
Leitung von Hermann Maurer

Restaurorische Betreuung: Christoph Bueble

Gestaltung: Karlheinz Rau, München
Aktualisierung und Umschlag: Erasmi & Stein, München

Katalog- und Drucksachenkoordianation: Norbert Brey

Fotonachweis siehe Seite 147
Umschlagmotiv Vorderseite: Red Kings, 1981 (Seite 53)
Rückseite: Defensive Orange, Offensive Orange, 1982
(Seite 60/61)

Lithographie und Druck: EBS
Editoriale Bortolazzi Stei s. r. l., Verona

Aktualisierte und veränderte Auflage:
© 2001 Museum Würth und Swiridoff Verlag, Künzelsau

Erste Auflage:
© 1999 Museums-Betriebs-Gesellschaft mbH,
Wien für KunstHausWien

© der abgebildeten Werke VG Bild-Kunst, Bonn 2001

Printed and bound in Italy

ISBN 3-934350-56-9

The exhibition »Jean Michel Basquiat – The Mugrabi Collection« gives the Würth Museum the opportunity to present to the public at large a private collection so far unknown in Germany and at the same time a retrospective of an artist's work.

First and foremost I would like to thank Prof. Dr. h.c. Reinhold Würth for taking the initiative and José Mugrabi for his readiness to loan the collection to us. The commitment of these two gentlemen allows us to present approximately 90 examples of Basquiat's work; some exhibits by Andy Warhol, a close friend of Basquiat, taken from the Würth Collection, will complement the exhibition in Künzelsau.

Basquiat was born in Brooklyn in 1960 to a Puerto Rican mother and a Haitian father. In the international art scene of the 1980s he experienced a meteoric rise and was already world famous when he died in 1988. In the fight against discrimination, violence and intolerance, Basquiat champions equality and human rights, something that is reflected in his work just like the seemingly naive scenes taken from an intact world.

After Basquiat's death, exhibitions in the U.S., in Europe, and here predominantly in France and Italy, as well as in Africa and Japan apart from accompanying films keep the Basquiat legend alive: the shooting star of the art scene, the autodidact highly acclaimed as genius who left the life as black street kid behind, a life that he had chosen himself, to become a musician and graffiti artist and following that a self-assured »avant-garde gallery painter«. However, in the barely ten years of his career, Basquiat does not see his recurrent codes and symbols being analytically decoded. His work that comprises roughly 1,000 paintings, numerous objects and 2,000 works on paper is rather placed in the tradition of western European and American art, a fact that ignored the entirety of Basquiat's artistic influences. Art experts recognized the effect that both Jean Dubuffet and Cy Twombly had on Basquiat's work and ranked the artist with the neo-expressive movement of the 80s. And yet, one can only do justice to Basquiat's work if one interprets it in the context of his Afro-American cultural heritage, something that was corroborated both by an exhibition in the New York Whitney Museum of American Art in 1992 and by more recent research.

Our exhibition is therefore not only intended as exciting overview of Basquiat's work, we rather want to offer a more in-depth insight through a broad range of accompanying events such as lectures and films.

I would like to thank everybody who helped in putting together the exhibition in Künzelsau. I particularly thank the entire team of the Würth Museum who has been showing outstanding commitment in the year of the opening of Kunsthalle Würth in Schwäbisch Hall. Without this commitment our exhibitions and accompanying events in another location would simply not have been possible. I am very grateful, too, to all the people who supported this exhibition either by supplying information or by active participation, namely Esty Neuman, Charles Danziger, Thaddaeus Ropac, Jacob Baal-Teshuva, Maripol, Susanna Reich, Susanne Reichling, the office of Erasmi & Stein, everybody who helped with the catalog, the Swiridoff publishing house and Carla Bassermann. I also thank all those very much who always show great interest in our activities and remain loyal to our now two museums. We are very happy to be able to bring another special highlight to Künzelsau with the Basquiat exhibition and are very much looking forward to your visit!

C. Sylvia Weber,
Director of the Kunsthalle und Museum Würth, 2001

Inhalt
Contents

Jacob Baal-Teshuva | **11** | Vorwort
Foreword

Richard Rodriguez | **15** | Jean Michel Basquiat

Henry Geldzahler | **19** | Von der U-Bahn nach Soho
From Subways to Soho
Jean Michel Basquiat

Jeffrey Hoffeld | **27** | Basquiat und der innere Mensch
Basquiat and the inner self

Jeffrey Hoffeld | **32** | Basquiat und die Unterirdischen
Basquiat and the Subterraneans

Jeffrey Deitch | **37** | Jean Michel Basquiat
Eine Hommage
An Homage

A. R. Penck | **41** | Poem for J.M. Basquiat

Francesco Clemente | **42** | Für Jean Michel
For Jean Michel

Francesco Clemente | **45** | Für Diego
For Diego

47 | **Katalog**
Catalogue

147 | **Fotonachweis**
Photo Credits

150 | **Biographie**
Chronology

165 | **Ausstellungen**
Exhibitions

171 | **Bibliographie**
Bibliography

172 | **Videos und Filme**
Videos and Films

Vorwort

»Jean Michel lebte wie eine Flamme. Er brannte lichterloh. Dann erlosch das Feuer. Aber die Glut ist noch immer heiß.« Mit diesen schönen, sehr poetischen Worten faßte sein langjähriger Freund Fred Braithwaite, besser unter dem Namen Fab Freddy 5 bekannt, die tragisch kurze, aufregende und stürmische Karriere der bedeutendsten Erscheinung der New Yorker Kunstszene der achtziger Jahre zusammen.

Jean Michel Basquiat war der erste schwarz-hispanische Superstar-Künstler, eine Bezeichnung, die auf Andy Warhol zurückgeht, der sein enger Freund wurde, sein Guru und, später, Mitstreiter des jungen Künstlers, als sie gemeinsam Gemälde ausführten.

Basquiat war nur 27 Jahre alt, als seine kurze, glänzende und vielversprechende Laufbahn auf tragische Weise – durch eine Überdosis von Drogen – beendet wurde.

Basquiat, Sohn einer puertoricanischen Mutter und eines haitianischen Vaters, begann schon im zartesten Alter zu zeichnen. Nach der Trennung der Eltern ist er etliche Male von zu Hause weggelaufen und ging auch ohne Abschluß von der »High School for Gifted Children« ab, um Künstler zu werden. Er war fest entschlossen, ein erfolgreicher Künstler und reich und berühmt wie Andy Warhol zu werden. Er sagte, »Seit ich siebzehn war, glaubte ich, ich könnte ein Star werden …«. »Papa,« sagte er einmal zu seinem Vater, »ich werde eines Tages sehr sehr berühmt.«

Und sehr berühmt wurde er auch, mit mehreren Museumsausstellungen in der ganzen Welt und einem Spielfilm über sein Leben, »Basquiat«, der international zu sehen war. Er hat es nicht mehr erlebt, daß bei Versteigerungen seine Gemälde – wie in jüngster Zeit – für über drei Millionen Dollar von Museen und Sammlern erworben wurden. Sein erstes Bild verkaufte er für $ 100.

Basquiat wurde zuerst durch die Sprühdose bekannt: Seine Graffiti auf den Mauern und U-Bahn-Zügen Manhattans erregten einige Aufmerksamkeit. Er kombinierte Worte und Symbole auf raffinierte und witzige Weise und mit beißendem Humor. Dies waren gemeinsame Unternehmungen mit seinem Schulkameraden Al Diaz. Er zeichnete die Graffiti mit dem Namen »Samo« (Same old shit), eine von ihm erfundene Persönlichkeit, die ihren Lebensunterhalt damit verdiente, Ersatzreligion an den Mann zu bringen. 1979 kam es zum Bruch mit dem alten Freund, und er beschloß, den Namen Samo fallenzulassen. So sprühte er auf die Mauern von Soho und der East Village überall die Worte »Samo ist tot«. Basquiat, der seine Graffiti natürlich nicht verkaufen konnte, begann dann auf Leinwand zu malen und auf Papier zu zeichnen; das konnte er verkaufen. Er wurde über Nacht zum Erfolg.

Seine Karriere umspannte neun Jahre. Im Alter von 21 Jahren wurde er der jüngste Künstler, der, neben weiteren bekannten Künstlern, jemals zur Teilnahme an der renommierten Documenta in Kassel aufgefordert worden ist.

Foreword

»Jean Michel lived like a flame. He burned really bright. Then the fire went out. But the embers are still hot.« With these beautiful and poetic words his long time friend Fred Braithwaite, better known as Fab 5 Freddy, sums up the tragically short lived exciting and tumulteous career of one of the most important figures of the New York art scene of the eighties.

Jean Michel Basquiat became the first black-hispanic superstar artist, a term coined by Andy Warhol, who became a close friend, his guru and later a collaborator of the young artist, when they worked jointly on paintings.

Basquiat was only 27 years old, when his short, bright and promising career came to a tragic end in 1988, as a result of an overdose of drugs.

Basquiat, who was born to a Puerto-Rican mother and a Haitian father, started drawing at a very early age. He ran away from home several times, after his parents' separation and later dropped out of high school for gifted children, in order to become an artist. In his heart he was determined to become a successful artist, and like Andy Warhol, rich and famous. He said, »Since I was seventeen I thought I might be a star...«. »Papa«, once Basquiat said to his father, »I will be very very famous one day.«

And very famous he became, with several museum exhibitions the world over, and a feature film on his life, »Basquiat«, playing in movie houses internationally. He did not live to see his paintings acquired lately by museums and collectors and bringing in auctions over three million dollars. He sold his first painting for $ 100.

Basquiat gained first notoriety and attention with his colour spray can, when he sprayed walls and subway trains in downtown Manhattan with graffiti. He combined words and symbols, full of wit and biting humour with his comments in a very sophisticated way. He did it together with his school friend, Al Diaz. He signed the graffiti with the name »Samo« (Same old shit), who makes a living selling fake religion. In 1979, he broke up with his friend and decided to abandon the name »Samo« by spraying the walls of Soho and east village with »Samo is dead«. Basquiat, who could not sell the graffiti on walls, started painting on canvas and drawing on paper, which he could sell. He became an overnight success.

His career spanned nine years. At the age of 21, he became the youngest artist ever to be invited to be exhibited with known artists at the famous Documenta in Kassel, Germany. His art became sought after by collectors and museums. Up to his tragic death in 1988, he had 37 exhibitions in galleries in Europe, Japan and the United States.

Basquiat was influenced in his work by poets, writers and jazz musicians, the then known »Beat Generation«. They were the poets Allen Ginsberg and William Borroughs,

Seine Kunst wurde bei Sammlern und Museen immer begehrter. Bis zu seinem tragischen Tod 1988 hatten 27 Ausstellungen in Galerien Europas, Japans und den Vereinigten Staaten stattgefunden.

Basquiat wurde in seinen Werken von Dichtern, Schriftstellern und Jazzmusikern der damals bekannten Beat-Generation beeinflußt. Das waren u. a. die Dichter Allen Ginsberg und William Burroughs und der Schriftsteller Jack Kerouac. Basquiat war auch ein begabter Musiker – er spielte Klarinette und Saxophon – und musizierte in mehreren Formationen mit. Er liebte Jazz und schwarze Starmusiker wie Charlie Parker und Jimi Hendrix, die wie er große Improvisatoren waren. Er bewunderte auch schwarze Sportidole, die er oft malte. Aber vor allem bewunderte er Andy Warhol, der für ihn ein Vorbild darin war, wie man reich und berühmt wird. Basquiat verdiente viel Geld, das er gern beim Bewirten von Freunden mit gutem Essen und Wein ausgab oder für Kleidung von Armani, die immer mit Farbklecksen besudelt war. Er war überaus großzügig und pflegte Obdachlosen einen Zwanzig-Dollar-Schein zu schenken.

Seine Thematik, sagte Basquiat 1985, seien »Könige, Helden und die Straße«. Die Krone war ein häufiges Motiv; sie wurde zu seinem Markenzeichen. Im Grunde wollte er »König der Künstler« werden. Nach seinem Tod malte Keith Haring ein Bild mit lauter Kronen, als Hommage an den Freund. In der damals von Weißen beherrschten Kunstszene machte Basquiat einen bedeutenden Durchbruch, weil auch er darin eine wichtige Rolle spielte.

In seiner kurzen, kometenhaften Karriere soll er 1000 Gemälde und etwa 2000 Zeichnungen hervorgebracht haben.

Obwohl er aufgehört hatte, Graffiti auf Mauern zu sprühen, enthielten auch seine Gemälde und Zeichnungen viele Worte und Symbole. Auf der Leinwand und dem Papier reagierte er auf tägliche Ereignisse, Rassenfragen, sein afrikanisches Kulturerbe und dessen Tradition und auf soziopolitische Themen. Seine Gemälde drückten auch seinen Zorn im Kampf der Schwarzen für Gleichheit und Menschenrechte aus. Seine Gemälde und Arbeiten auf Papier spielten weiters auf Themen aus der Kunstgeschichte an.

In seinem Werk sind Einflüsse und Anregungen der Graffiti Jean Dubuffets und Cy Twomblys, von Picasso, DeKooning und Franz Kline präsent, den Basquiat als einen seiner Lieblingskünstler bezeichnete. Jean Michel Basquiat war sehr empfindlich, wenn die Presse ihn kritisierte. Manche nannten ihn einen »Primitivkünstler« oder gar ein »Federgewicht«. Er wurde auch zum »Warhol-Maskottchen« oder »Eddie Murphy der Kunstszene« abgestempelt. In den achtziger Jahren stellte so mancher seine Kunst in Frage: »Ist das Kunst oder Vandalismus?« Es verletzte ihn sehr, wenn die Presse über seinen extravaganten Charakter und Lebensstil herzog, anstatt über seine Kunst zu schreiben, oder wenn manche Kritiker seine Kunst als Schwindel, »Hype« oder »niedrige Kunst«

author Jack Kerouac and others. Being a talented musician, playing the clarinet and saxophone, Basquiat participated in forming music bands. He adored Jazz and black star musicians, such as Charlie Parker and Jimi Hendrix, who, like him, used improvisations. He also admired black sport figures, whom he painted often. But most of all he admired Andy Warhol, who was for him a role model for becoming rich and famous. Basquiat earned lots of money, which he freely spent on friends with good food and wine, and Armani clothes, which were always splattered with paint. He was very generous and used to tip homeless people with $ 20 bills.

His subject matter, said Basquiat in 1985, was: »Royalty, heroism and the streets«. He painted very often crowns, which became his trade mark. Deep down in his heart he wanted to become »King of the artists«. After his death, as homage to Basquiat, Keith Haring produced a painting full of crowns, as a tribute to his friend. In the then dominant art scene of white male artists, Basquiat made a significant breakthrough, by becoming an important player on the art scene.

In his short meteoric career, he is said to have painted 1000 paintings and about 2000 drawings.

Although he stopped painting graffiti on walls, his canvases and drawings continue to have lots of words and symbols. He reacted on canvas and paper to daily events, race issues, his African culture and heritage and on socio-political subjects. His canvases also reflected and expressed anger in the fight of black people for equality and human rights. His canvases and works on paper also referred to art historical subjects.

One sees in his works influences and inspirations of Jean Dubuffet and Cy Twombley's graffiti, Picasso, DeKooning, and Franz Kline, whom Basquiat said, was one of his favorites. Jean Michel Basquiat was very sensitive to criticism of the press. Some called him a »primitive« or a »feather weight«. He was called a »Warhol mascot« or »the Eddie Murphy of the art world«. Some questioned during the eighties his work, asking, »Is it art or vandalism?« He was easily hurt when the press wrote about his flamboyant personality and behaviour and less about his art or when his work was called by some critics a hoax and hype or »low art«. He loved films and many influenced and inspired his work. He even appeared as the main figure in a film »New York Beat« by his friend Glenn O'Brien.

Basquiat, who opened doors for other black artists, said, »I don't even know if I want to be called a black painter, I just want to be me... I don't know if the fact that I am black has something to do with my success.«

Basquiat, together with Keith Haring, Kenny Scharf, Julian Schnabel, David Salle, Francesco Clemente and others, was one of the most talented and very exciting artists of the eighties in New York, recognized as such internationally.

abtaten. Er liebte den Film, und viele Filme haben sein Werk beeinflußt und angeregt. Er hat sogar in dem Film »New York Beat« seines Freundes Glenn O'Brien die Hauptrolle gespielt.

Basquiat, der für andere schwarze Künstler Türen geöffnet hat, sagte: »Ich weiß nicht einmal, ob ich ein schwarzer Maler genannt werden will, ich will nur ich sein.... Ich weiß nicht, ob die Tatsache, daß ich schwarz bin, etwas mit meinem Erfolg zu tun hat.«

Basquiat gilt international neben Keith Haring, Kenny Scharf, Julian Schnabel, David Salle, Francesco Clemente u. a. als einer der begabtesten und aufregendsten Künstler im New York der achtziger Jahre.

Basquiat beschäftigte sich in seinem Werk intensiv mit dem Tod, genau wie sein enger Freund Andy Warhol, der in seinen Gemälden Katastrophen, Autounfälle, Selbstmord, den elektrischen Stuhl und Porträts von Jacqueline Kennedy am Tage der Ermordung ihres Mannes im Jahre 1963 abgebildet hat. Basquiat glaubte nicht, daß er lange leben würde, vor allem nach dem Tod Andy Warhols im Jahre 1987. Die Todesthematik war in seinem breitgefächerten Œuvre vielfach vertreten: in Gemälden, Zeichnungen, Collagen, Siebdrucken und Plastiken.

Eines seiner letzten Gemälde, »Riding with Death«, ging auf eine Zeichnung von Leonardo da Vinci zurück. In diesem Bild scheint die schwarze, skeletähnliche Figur ihn selbst darzustellen: Sie ist unvollendet, fällt auseinander – genau wie sein Leben. Die Todesthematik erinnerte Basquiat oft an den Tod seines Mentors Andy Warhol. Er war ein Vorbote seines eigenen baldigen Todes.

Am 12. August 1988 fand sein Leben auf tragische Weise ein Ende: Basquiat wurde in seiner New Yorker Wohnung tot aufgefunden, gestorben an einer Überdosis von Drogen. In der Epoche der Beat-Generation, der er angehörte, hatte sein junges Herz aufgehört zu schlagen.

Seine Kunst wird in den kommenden Jahren weiterhin ausgestellt und diskutiert werden, man wird darüber schreiben und sie im Film zeigen, wie im erfolgreichen Spielfilm »Basquiat«, bei dem Julian Schnabel Regie führte.

Basquiat, der Autodidakt, – aufgeweckt, intelligent und sehr ehrgeizig – war ein Naturtalent, das in einer kurzen Karriere ein außerordentlich bemerkenswertes Werkcorpus hinterlassen hat, das seine Zeit, die achtziger Jahre, widerspiegelt, denen sein kurzer Erfolg selbst zum Opfer gefallen ist.

Jacob Baal-Teshuva
Februar 1999

Basquiat was very much involved in his work with the subject of death, like his close friend, Andy Warhol, who created paintings of disasters, car crashes, suicide, the electric chair and portraits of Jacqueline Kennedy on the day her husband, president Kennedy, was killed in 1963. Basquiat did not believe he will live long, especially after the death of Andy Warhol in 1987. The subject of death was quite evident in his wide range of work: paintings, drawings, collages, silkscreens and three-dimensional objects.

One of his very last paintings, »Riding with death«, was based on a drawing by Leonardo da Vinci. In the painting, the black skeleton figure seems to represent himself, unfinished, falling apart, like his life. The subject of death reminded him often of the death of his mentor Andy Warhol, who died in 1987. It was a premonition of his own nearing death.

On 12 August 1988, his short life came to a tragic end, when he was found dead in his appartement in New York, from an overdose of drugs. In the age of the Beat Generation, of which he was a part, his young heart stopped beating.

His art will, for years to come, continue to be exhibited, discussed, written about and shown in films, like the successful feature »Basquiat«, directed by Julian Schnabel.

Basquiat, who was self-taught, bright, intelligent and very ambitious, was a natural genius, who left in his short career a very remarkable body of work, which reflected his time during the eighties, of which he was a victim of his short lived success.

Jacob Baal-Teshuva
February 1999

Richard Rodriguez

Jean Michel Basquiat

»Man ersetzt nicht die Vergangenheit, man fügt ihr lediglich ein neues Glied hinzu.«
(Cézanne, Brief an Roger Marx, 23. Januar 1905).

Basquiat! Ein Name wie ein Peitschenknall in der Geschichte der Kunst am Ende des Jahrtausends.

Für manche ein Modephänomen, für andere ein echtes Genie – im Fall Jean Michel Basquiats bleibt niemand gleichgültig.

Es sind nun zehn Jahre her, seit er tragischerweise durch eine Überdosis dahingegangen ist, am 12. August 1988 im Alter von 27 Jahren.

Als emblematische Gestalt der amerikanischen Kunstszene der achtziger Jahre wurde seine Persönlichkeit in den Medien verzerrt und karikiert, aber der vollendete Künstler, der er schon immer war, setzte sich letztlich doch durch.

Sein Œuvre erweist sich trotz der kurzen Entstehungsperiode als bedeutsam, quantitativ und vor allem qualitativ, und nimmt in der piktoralen Geschichte des nun endenden 20. Jahrhunderts eine Spitzenstellung ein.

Es ist unvermeidlich, daß für die Nachwelt die achtziger Jahre die Jahre Basquiats sein werden.

In der Tat ist das Werk eines Künstlers selten derart identisch mit seiner Epoche und ein solches Spiegelbild einer Generation geworden, die auf dem Altar des Profits geopfert wurde.

Drogen, Aids, Rassismus, Intoleranz, Gewalt, Umweltverschmutzung, soziale Misere, Kulturschock … alle diese Übel unserer Jahrtausendwende spiegeln sich auf bewundernswerte Weise im Werk Basquiats wider; es verkündet sie mit einer Kraft, einer Originalität und beispielhaften Authentizität.

Als Wunderkind und verlorener Sohn zugleich starb er in einem Alter, in dem die meisten Künstler gerade ihre gestalterische Reife erreichen, und dennoch hat er ein abgeschlossenes Œuvre hinterlassen. Gleich zu Beginn seiner künstlerischen Karriere, mit 20 Jahren, war sein Stil imponierend – selten hat ein Künstler von einer so außerordentlich frühen kreativen Reife profitieren können.

»… Seine Persönlichkeit war widersprüchlich: von außergewöhnlicher Intelligenz und phänomenaler Begabung war er gleichzeitig naiv und kleinbürgerlich und imstande, sich wie ein kleines Kind über eine Lappalie zu freuen.

Andererseits hatte er einen Hang zum Dandyhaften und liebte es im Leben den Komfort und Luxus zu genießen, wie nur das Geld es ermöglicht.

Richard Rodriguez

Jean Michel Basquiat

»There is no substitution for the past, one can only add another link to it.«
(Cézanne in a letter to Roger Marx, January 23, 1905)

Basquiat! A name like a crack of the whip in art at the close of the millennium.

A fad for some, for others a true genius: in Jean Michel Basquiat's case nobody remains indifferent.

It has been ten years now since he tragically passed away from an overdose, on August 12, 1988, at the age of 27.

This emblematic figure in the American art scene of the eighties was extremely distorted and caricatured in the sensationalist media, but the mature artist he had always been finally established his reputation anyway.

Despite the short time of its creation, his œuvre has proven to be significant, quantitatively and, even more so, qualitatively, and ranks as one of the leading body of pictures in the 20th century as it nears its close.

It is unevitable that for posterity, the eighties will be the years of Basquiat.

Indeed, the work of an artist has seldom been so closely identified with his epoch and such a mirror reflection of a generation sacrificed on the altar of profit.

Drugs, AIDS, racism, intolerance, violence, pollution, social squalor, cultural shock... all these evils of the turn of the millennium are admirably echoed in Basquiat's work and heralded with a power, an originality, and exemplary authenticity.

A child prodigy and prodigal son all in one, he died at an age at which most artists are just achieving their creative maturity, and yet he has left a well rounded work behind, all the same. At the outset of his artistic career, at age twenty, his style was impressive – rarely has an artist been in the position of benefitting from such extraordinary early maturity.

»… He had a contradictory personality: of exceptional intelligence, endowed with phenomenal talent, he was naive and bourgeois at the same time, capable of waxing enthusiastic over trifles like a small child.

On the other hand, he had a penchant for dandyism and loved to live in the sumptuous surroundings and luxury which only money could procure.

He was particularly vain, as can be seen in the photographs we have of him; even for a snapshot he struck a pose.

One can definitely ascribe the great number of works he executed during his short life to this vanity, that is, to this need for social recognition.

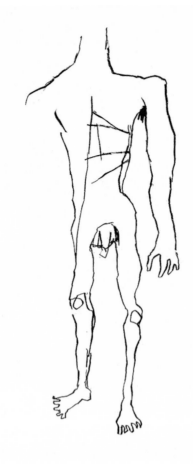

Jean Michel Basquiat, Anatomy Six, 1983
Kohle auf Papier 76 x 56 cm

Er war insbesondere eitel, wie man auf den erhaltenen Fotos feststellen kann; selbst bei Gelegenheitsaufnahmen nahm er stets eine Pose ein.

Es ist diese Eitelkeit, die letztlich ein Bedürfnis nach gesellschaftlicher Anerkennung war und der man die große Zahl der Werke verdankt, die er in seinem kurzen Leben ausgeführt hat.

Seine vorurteilslose und überspannte Natur hinterließ den Eindruck einer unzufriedenen Randexistenz.

Ein Geisteszustand ohne jede Absicherung gegen die Probleme des inneren Daseins führte dazu, daß er diese Themen ohne Umschweife und Zurückhaltung behandelte.

Er interessierte sich vor allem für die Kunst. Er war auf künstlerische Fragen – und sich selbst – total fixiert. Sich seiner Begabung voll bewußt, hat er nie gezweifelt, daß früher oder später die Welt sein Genie anerkennen würde.

Schon als Kind zeichnete er stundenlang und war nur vor Papier und Farbstiften glücklich. Selbst in der Schule hat ihn sonst nichts interessiert...«

Diese Charakterisierung Egon Schieles, die jener Jean Michel Basquiats erstaunlich ähnlich ist, wurde vom unvergessenen Serge Sabarsky für einen Katalog einer Schiele-Ausstellung geschrieben.

His prejudice-free, exalted nature left the impression of an unsatisfied marginal existence.

A state of mind with no safeguards as to the problems of the inner self caused him to treat these topics directly, with no holds barred.

He was interested above all in art. He was entirely concentrated on artistic questions – and himself. Fully conscious of his gifts, he never doubted that sooner or later the world would recognize his genius.

Even as a child, he spent hours drawing and was only happy in front of a sheet of paper and color pencils. Even at school nothing else interested him ...«

This description of Egon Schiele, which so astonishingly resembles that of Jean Michel Basquiat, was written by the late Serge Sabarsky for the catalogue of one of his exhibitions.

It is troubling to see, despite the space of seventy years and all the differences in social origins which separate them, such a similarity in their personalities, their talent, their fate.

Indeed, these prodigal children have more than one thing in common:

Both loved to draw from earliest childhood with an unusual intensity, with incisive, powerful strokes, playing

Es hat etwas Beunruhigendes, in einem Abstand von siebzig Jahren und bei aller Unterschiedlichkeit der Herkunft, eine derartige Ähnlichkeit der Persönlichkeit, des Talents und des Schicksals zu konstatieren.

In der Tat verbindet mehr als eine Gemeinsamkeit diese beiden Wunderkinder:

Sie hatten beide von frühester Kindheit an eine übermäßige Freude am Zeichnen. Sie führten die Zeichnungen mit sicheren, energischen Zügen aus, wobei sie in einem Spiel mit den weißen Flächen des Papiers das Sujet aus dem Rahmen hoben oder absichtlich unvollendet ließen.

Beide hatten eine tiefe persönliche Beziehung zu einem »geistigen Vater«: Klimt bei Schiele, Warhol bei Basquiat.

Aufgrund ihres Nonkonformismus und ihrer subversiven Grundeinstellung waren sie der gesellschaftlichen Ablehnung und Kritik ihrer Zeit ausgesetzt, genossen aber dennoch die Unterstützung einflußreicher Persönlichkeiten aus der Welt der Kunst.

Sie sind praktisch im gleichen Alter gestorben, nur wenige Monate auseinander: Schiele mit 28, Basquiat mit 27, im vollen Ruhm hinweggerafft; aber trotz allem, dank ihrer Frühreife und verschwenderischen Begabung, hinterließen sie ein bedeutendes Œuvre von großer Originalität.

Beide gehören zu den genialen Malern, die die »Glieder« der künstlerischen Kette des 20. Jahrhunderts ausmachen, jeweils an entgegengesetzten Enden, am Beginn und am virtuosen Ausgang dieses hervorragenden Jahrhunderts in der Kunstgeschichte.

Alle diese Gemeinsamkeiten konnten nur dazu führen, daß sie sich eines Tages in Wien begegnen sollten.

Richard Rodriguez ist Sammler und Experte für das Werk von Jean Michel Basquiat in Paris.

with the blank spaces on the paper, taking the subject beyond the allotted space or intentionally leaving it unfinished.

Both had a deep affectionate relationship with a »spiritual father«: Klimt for Schiele and Andy Warhol for Basquiat.

Due to their non-conformism and their subversive attitude, they were subject to the opprobrium and criticism of the society of their period, but nonetheless benefitted from the support of influential personalities in modern art.

They died practically at the same age: Schiele at 28, Basquiat at 27, whisked from the scene at their full glory; but in spite of all, thanks to their precociousness and prodigality, leaving an important oeuvre of great originality behind.

Both belong to those ingenious painters who form the »links« in the chain of art in the 20th century, each at one end of it, at the beginning and the virtuose end of this outstanding century in the history of art.

All these common traits could only result in their meeting one day in Vienna.

Richard Rodriguez is a collector, and expert on the work of Jean Michel Basquiat, in Paris.

Henry Geldzahler

Von der U-Bahn nach Soho
Jean Michel Basquiat

1976 begann Jean Michel Basquiat, unter dem Namen SAMO seine einzigartigen Graffiti in ganz Manhattan zu »schreiben«. Von Anfang an bestand sein Werk aus konzeptionell verschlüsselten Verbindungen von Worten und Symbolen in der lapidaren Einfachheit spätrömischer Inschriften. Nachdem er von U-Bahn-Mauern zur Leinwand und von den Straßen New Yorks zu den Galerien Sohos avanciert war, eroberte Basquiat Anfang 1982 die Kunstszene im Sturm mit einer fulminanten Einzelausstellung in der Annina Nosei Gallery. Seine erste Einzelausstellung überhaupt fand allerdings und vielleicht ironischerweise nicht in New York, sondern in Italien, in Modena, statt. Seitdem fanden Ausstellungen u.a. bei der Documenta 7 und in der New Yorker Fun Gallery statt.

Henry Geldzahler: *Haben Sie sich als Graffitikünstler empfunden, noch bevor diese Bezeichnung zum bürgerlichen Luxus geworden ist?*

Jean Michel Basquiat: Ich glaube ja.

HG: *Haben Sie deshalb in den Straßen und der U-Bahn gearbeitet, weil Sie nichts hatten, worauf Sie malen konnten oder weil Sie etwas mitteilen wollten?*

JMB: Ich wollte mir einen Namen machen.

HG: *Und ein Revier? Hatten Sie ein Gebiet, das Ihnen gehörte?*

JMB: Meistens »downtown«. Und die Linie »D«.

HG: *Wie kamen Sie auf die Linie »D«?*

JMB: Damit fuhr ich nach Hause, von downtown nach Brooklyn.

HG: *Aber Sie wußten von Anfang an, daß Brooklyn nicht Ihre Malfläche sein würde. Die Kunst fand in Manhattan statt, und dort würden Sie also arbeiten?*

JMB: Naja, SAMO sollte eigentlich nicht »Kunst« sein.

HG: *Welche Materialien benutzten Sie?*

JMB: Einen schwarzen Lackstift.

HG: *Egal worauf? Oder auf etwas, das vorher präpariert, gestaltet worden war?*

JMB: Die Graffiti? Nein, das fand unmittelbar auf der Straße statt.

HG: *Hatten Sie irgendwie daran gedacht, einen Durchbruch zur Kunstszene zu schaffen?*

JMB: Nein.

HG: *Aber als ich Sie sah, waren Sie etwa 17 Jahre alt. Sie zeigten mir Zeichnungen, das war vor vier, fünf Jahren... Ich war im Restaurant, im WPA, in Soho.*

Henry Geldzahler

Art: from subways to Soho
Jean Michel Basquiat

In 1976, Jean Michel Basquiat began »writing« his unique brand of graffiti throughout Manhattan under the name »SAMO«. His work from the first consisted of conceptual, enigmatic combinations of words and symbols, executed with the curt simplicity of a late Roman inscription. Graduating from subway walls to canvas and from the streets of New York to the galleries of Soho, Basquiat took the art world by storm with his rampageous one man show at Annina Nosei's gallery, early in 1982. His first one man show, perhaps ironically, was not in New York, but in Italy, in Modena. Exhibitions since then have included Documenta 7 and the Fun Gallery, New York.

Henry Geldzahler: *Did you ever think of yourself as a graffiti artist, before the name became a middle class luxury?*

Jean Michel Basquiat: I guess I did.

HG: *Did you work in the streets and subways because you didn't have materials or because you wanted to communicate?*

JMB: I wanted to build up a name for myself.

HG: *Territory? Did you have an area that was yours?*

JMB: Mostly downtown. Then the »D« train.

HG: *How'd you pick the »D« train?*

JMB: That was the one I went home on, from downtown to Brooklyn.

HG: *But you knew Brooklyn wasn't going to be your canvas from the beginning. Manhattan was where the art goes on, so that was where you were going to work?*

JMB: Well, SAMO wasn't supposed to be art, really.

HG: *What were the materials?*

JMB: Black magic marker.

HG: *On anything? Or something that was already prepared and formed?*

JMB: The graffiti? No, that was right on the streets.

HG: *Did you have any idea about breaking into the art world?*

JMB: No.

HG: *But when I saw you, you were about 17 years old. You were showing me drawings, that was 4 or 5 years ago ... I was in the restaurant, WPA, in Soho.*

JMB: Yeah, I remember.

HG: *So you already had work to show.*

JMB: Ja, ich erinnere mich.

HG: *Sie hatten also schon damals vorzeigbare Arbeit.*

JMB: Nein, ich verkaufte diese Postkarten, und jemand hat mir gesagt, Sie wären gerade in dieses Restaurant hineingegangen. Erst nach etwa 15 Minuten habe ich mich getraut, Ihnen nachzugehen. Ich ging hinein, und Sie sagten: »Zu jung!« Und da ging ich wieder.

HG: *Grausam, aber wahr.*

JMB: Zu dem Zeitpunkt traf es zu.

HG: *Waren Sie wütend?*

JMB: Ein bißchen schon. Ich meine, zu jung wozu, verstehen Sie? Aber ich sah es ein: Sie wollten essen – »Wer ist denn dieser Junge überhaupt?«.

HG: *Die nächste Begegnung war über einem Kreditbüro am Eingang zur Manhattan-Brücke. Ich war sehr beeindruckt und besonders erstaunt vom Bild, das ich mit nach Hause nahm. Wird es auseinanderfallen? Soll ich es neu kleben lassen oder hinter Glas montieren?*

JMB: Ganz wie Sie wollen. Ein kleiner Goldrahmen tut's.

HG: *Wie haben Sie als Heranwachsender über die Kunst gedacht? Gingen Sie ins Brooklyn Museum?*

JMB: Ja, meine Mutter führte mich überall hin.

HG: *Hatten Sie irgendeine Vorstellung von Haitischer Kunst?*

JMB: Nein. Als ich noch jünger war, wollte ich Karikaturist werden.

HG: *Als ich Ihnen zum erstenmal begegnete, erwähnten Sie Franz Kline.*

JMB: Ja, er gehört zu meinen Lieblingskünstlern.

HG: *Mir ist zu Ohren gekommen, Sie hätten das Gerücht in die Welt gesetzt, daß Sie mit Julian Schnabel einen Boxkampf abhalten wollten.*

JMB: Das war bevor ich ihn kennengelernt hatte. Und dann kam er eines Tages in Anninas Galerie. Ich fragte ihn, ob er ein bißchen Sparring machen wollte.

HG: *Er ist ziemlich kräftig.*

JMB: Oh ja, fand ich auch. Aber ich dachte, selbst wenn ich verliere, würde ich keine schlechte Figur machen.

HG: *Wessen Gemälde mögen Sie besonders gern?*

JMB: Je mehr ich male, um so mehr gefällt mir alles Mögliche.

HG: *Haben Sie ein Gefühl der Hektik, daß Sie möglichst viel schaffen müssen?*

JMB: Nein, ich weiß bloß nicht, was ich sonst mit mir anfangen soll.

JMB: No, I was selling these postcards and somebody told me you had just gone into this restaurant. It took me about 15 minutes to get up the nerve to go in there. I went in and you said, »Too young.« And I left.

HG: *Cruel, but true.*

JMB: It was true at the time.

HG: *Were you furious?*

JMB: Sort of. I mean, too young for what, you know? But I could see, it was lunch time. »Who is this kid?«

HG: *The next time I saw you was about two years later above a loan shop at the entrance to the Manhattan Bridge. I was very impressed; I was amazed, especially by the picture I got. Is that going to fall apart? Should I have it restuck, or put it behind glass?*

JMB: Anything is fine. A little gold frame.

HG: *What was your idea of art as a kid? Did you go to the Brooklyn Museum?*

JMB: Yeah, my mother took me around a lot.

HG: *Did you have any idea what Haitian art was?*

JMB: No. I wanted to be a cartoonist when I was young.

HG: *When I first met you, you mentioned Franz Kline.*

JMB: Yeah, he's one of my favorites.

HG: *I heard you'd been spreading a rumor that you wanted to have a boxing match with Julian Schnabel.*

JMB: This was before I'd ever met him. And one day he came into Annina's gallery. And I asked him if he wanted to spar.

HG: *He's pretty strong.*

JMB: Oh yeah, I thought so. But I figured even if I lost, I couldn't look bad.

HG: *Whose paintings do you like?*

JMB: The more I paint the more I like everything.

HG: *Do you feel a hectic need to get a lot of work done?*

JMB: No. I just don't know what else to do with myself.

HG: *Painting is your activity, and that's what you do...*

JMB: Pretty much. A little socializing.

HG: *Do you still draw a lot?*

JMB: Yesterday was the first time I'd drawn in a long time. I'd been sort of living off this pile of drawings from last year, sticking them on paintings.

HG: *Are you drawing on good paper now or do you not care about that?*

JMB: For a while I was drawing on good paper, but now I've gone back to the bad stuff. I put matte medium on it.

HG: *Die Malerei ist Ihre Beschäftigung, das führen Sie aus...*

JMB: So ziemlich. Und ein bißchen unter die Leute gehen.

HG: *Zeichnen Sie noch viel?*

JMB: Gestern habe ich zum erstenmal seit langem wieder gezeichnet. Ich hatte gewissermaßen von diesem Stapel Zeichnungen aus dem letzten Jahr gelebt, indem ich sie auf meine Gemälde aufklebte.

HG: *Zeichnen Sie jetzt auf gutem Papier oder ist Ihnen das egal?*

JMB: Eine Zeitlang zeichnete ich auf gutem Papier, aber jetzt bin ich zum schlechten Zeug zurückgekehrt. Ich trage eine Mattpaste auf, die es versiegelt, und dann ist das Papier egal.

HG: *Mir ist in Ihren jüngsten Arbeiten aufgefallen, daß Sie zur Haltung zurückgekehrt sind, daß die Verteilung im Bild sekundär ist; ein Teil der Arbeiten scheint recht zufällig verteilt...*

JMB: Alles ist ausgewogen, auch wenn es anders erscheinen mag.

HG: *Alle Künstler oder Kunstströmungen – sobald sie zur Einfachheit, zu den Grundlagen vorstoßen wollen – verbannen zeitweilig die Farbe, um später zu ihr zurückzukehren. Die Farbe ist die Rokokobühne, und Schwarzweiß das nackte konstruierte Knochengerüst. In Ihrer Arbeit schwanken Sie sehr häufig hin und her. Ist Ihnen das aufgefallen?*

JMB: Davon weiß ich nichts.

HG: *Wenn die Farbe zu schön wird, weichen Sie wieder zurück – zu etwas Zornigerem, Grundlegenderem...*

JMB: Mir gefallen jene Arbeiten, wo ich nicht so viel male wie bei anderen, wo sich einfach eine unmittelbare Idee zeigt.

HG: *Wie das, was ich hier bei mir habe.*

JMB: Ja. Ich glaube nicht, daß noch etwas unter der Goldfarbe steckt. Die meisten Bilder haben ein, zwei Gemälde darunter. Ich mache mir Sorgen, daß später Teile vielleicht herunterfallen und Köpfe vom Untergrund zum Vorschein kommen könnten.

HG: *Sie werden wohl nicht herunterfallen, aber mit der Zeit verändert sich die Farbe. Viele Renaissance-Gemälde haben sogenannte »Pentimenti«. Das sind Veränderungen, bei denen ein darunter befindlicher »Phantom«-Kopf, der um fünf Grad verlagert ist, zum Vorschein kommt.*

JMB: Ich habe ein Gemälde, in dem jemand ein Huhn im Arm hält, und unter dem Huhn ist ein menschlicher Kopf.

HG: *Es wird nicht genau so herunterfallen. Das ganze Huhn fällt nicht herunter.*

JMB (lachend): Oh!

If you put matte medium on it, it seals it up, so it doesn't really matter.

HG: *I've noticed in the recent work you've gone back to the idea of not caring how well stretched it is; part of the work seems to be casual...*

JMB: Everything is well stretched even though it looks like it may not be.

HG: *All artists, or all art movements, when they want to simplify and get down to basics, eliminate color for a while, then go back to color. Color is the rococo stage, and black and white is the constructed, bare bones. You swing back and forth very quickly in your work. Are you aware of that?*

JMB: I don't know.

HG: *If the color gets too beautiful, you retreat from it to something angrier and more basic...*

JMB: I like the ones where I don't paint as much as others, where it's just a direct idea.

HG: *Like the one I have upstairs.*

JMB: Yeah. I don't think there's anything under that gold paint. Most of the pictures have one or two paintings under them. I'm worried that in the future, parts might fall off and some of the heads underneath might show through.

HG: *They might not fall off, but paint changes in time. Many Renaissance paintings have what's called »pentimenti,« changes where the »ghost« head underneath which was five degrees off will appear.*

JMB: I have a painting where somebody's holding a chicken, and underneath the chicken is somebody's head.

HG: *It won't fall off exactly like that. The whole chicken won't fall off.*

JMB (laughs): Oh.

HG: *Do you do self-portraits?*

JMB: Every once in a while, yeah.

HG: *Do you think your family is proud of you?*

JMB: Yeah, I guess so.

HG: *What did you think of James Van der Zee?*

JMB: Oh, he was really great. He has a great sense of the »good picture«.

HG: *What kind of a camera did he use?*

JMB: Old box camera that had a little black lens cap on the front that he'd take off to make the exposure, then put back on.

HG: *Do you find your personal life, your relationships with various women get into the work?*

HG: *Machen Sie auch Selbstbildnisse?*

JMB: Hin und wieder, ja.

HG: *Glauben Sie, daß Ihre Familie auf Sie stolz ist?*

JMB: Ja, ich glaube schon.

HG: *Was halten Sie von James Van der Zee?*

JMB: Oh, der war große Klasse. Er hat einen guten Sinn für das »gute« Bild.

HG: *Was für eine Kamera benutzte er?*

JMB: Einen alten Kasten mit einer kleinen schwarzen Kappe am Objektiv, die er zur Belichtung herunternahm und dann wieder aufsetzte.

HG: *Kommt es vor, daß sich Ihr Privatleben, Ihre Beziehungen mit verschiedenen Frauen in Ihrer Arbeit niederschlagen?*

JMB: Gelegentlich, wenn ich auf eine Frau wütend bin, mache ich ein großes, schreckliches Bild über sie...

HG: *Und sie weiß, daß sie das Thema ist, oder handelt es sich um eine Geheimsprache?*

JMB: Manchmal, manchmal auch nicht.

HG: *Machen Sie sie selbst darauf aufmerksam?*

JMB: Nein, manchmal ist es sogar mir selbst nicht klar.

HG: *Machen Ihre Freunde Sie darauf aufmerksam, oder wird es einfach mit der Zeit klar?*

JMB: Das sind jene kleinen Ikonen, die an die Zeit erinnern...

HG: *Indizien.*

JMB: Da war eine Frau, mit der ich damals Umgang hatte... Natürlich mochte ich sie nach einer Weile nicht mehr, und so begann ich, sie als Olympia zu malen. Und dann endlich machte ich Schluß mit ihr.

HG: *Mit wem kommt man schwerer aus, mit Freundinnen oder Kunsthändlern?*

JMB: Das ist eigentlich so ziemlich das Gleiche.

HG: *Hat es Ihnen Spaß gemacht, als Sie für Ihre erste Ausstellung, in Modena, nach Italien fuhren?*

JMB: Es hat Spaß gemacht, weil es das erste Mal war, aber finanziell war es ziemlich blöd.

HG: *Hat man Sie in die Pfanne gehauen?*

JMB: Ja, er hat ein richtiges Pauschalgeschäft gemacht.

HG: *Hat er die Bilder wieder verkauft? Sind sie irgendwo unterwegs in der Welt?*

JMB: Ich nehme es an.

JMB: Occasionally, when I get mad at a woman, I'll do some great, awful painting about her...

HG: *Which she knows is about her, or is it a private language?*

JMB: Sometimes. Sometimes not.

HG: *Do you point it out?*

JMB: No, sometimes I don't even know it.

HG: *Do friends point it out to you, or does it just become obvious as time goes on?*

JMB: It's just those little mental icons of the time...

HG: *Clues.*

JMB: There was a woman I went out with... I didn't like her after awhile of course, so I started painting her as Olympia. At the very end I cut the maid off.

HG: *Who's harder to get along with, girl-friends or dealers?*

JMB: They're about the same, actually.

HG: *Did you have a good time when you went to Italy, for the first show, in Modena?*

JMB: It was fun because it was the first time, but financially it was pretty stupid.

HG: *It was a rip-off?*

JMB: Yeah, he really got a bulk deal.

HG: *Has he re-sold them? Are they out in the world?*

JMB: I guess so.

HG: *Do you ever see them? Would you recognize them?*

JMB: I recognize them. I'm a little shocked when I see them.

HG: *Are there Italian words in them?*

JMB: Mostly skelly-courts and strike zones.

HG: *What's a skelly-court?*

JMB: It's a street game, with a grid.

HG: *What about the alchemical works, like tin and lead...*

JMB: I think that worked.

HG: *I think so, too.*

JMB: Because I was writing gold on all this stuff, and I made all this money right afterwards.

HG: *What about words like tin and asbestos?*

JMB: That's alchemy, too.

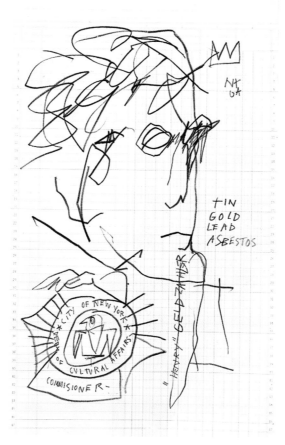

Jean Michel Basquiat, Henry Geldzahler, 1982
Kugelschreiber und Bleistift auf Papier   35,5 x 21,6 cm

HG: *Kriegen Sie sie je zu sehen? Würden Sie sie wieder-erkennen?*

JMB: Ich erkenne sie wieder. Es schockiert mich ein wenig, wenn ich sie sehe.

HG: *Enthalten sie italienische Wörter?*

JMB: Zumeist »Skelly«-Flächen und Streikzonen.

HG: *Was ist denn eine Skelly-Fläche?*

JMB: Das ist ein Straßenspiel, mit einem Rasterfeld.

HG: *Und dann die alchemistischen Arbeiten, mit Zinn und Blei...*

JMB: Ich glaube, das hat funktioniert.

HG: *Ich auch.*

JMB: Weil ich »Gold« auf alle diese Dinge geschrieben habe, und unmittelbar danach habe ich so viel Geld gemacht.

HG: *Und Worte wie »Zinn« und »Asbest«?*

JMB: Auch das ist Alchemie.

HG: *Und wie ist es mit der Liste der Vorsokratiker in den jüngsten Gemälden und die Materialien, die schon immer in Ihren Gemälden Eingang gefunden haben, die nicht so*

HG: *What about the list of pre-Socratic philosophers in the recent paintings, and the kinds of materials which get into your painting always, that derive not so much from Twombly, as from the same kind of synthetic thinking. Is that something you've done from your childhood, lists of things?*

JMB: That was from going to Italy, and copying names out of tour books, and condensed histories.

HG: *Is the impulse to know a lot, or is the impulse to copy out things that strike you?*

JMB: Well, originally I wanted to copy the whole history down, but it was too tedious so I just stuck to the cast of characters.

HG: *So they're kinds of indexes to encyclopedias that don't exist.*

JMB: I just like the names.

HG: *What is your subject matter?*

JMB (pause): Royalty, heroism, and the streets.

HG: *But your picture of the streets is improved by the fact that you've improved the streets.*

JMB: I think I have to give that crown to Keith Haring. I haven't worked in the streets in so long.

sehr von Twombly als von einem ähnlich synthetischen Denken herrühren? Ist das etwas, das Sie seit Ihrer Kindheit praktizieren: Sachen auflisten?

JMB: Das kam im Zusammenhang mit der Reise nach Italien auf: Ich schrieb Namen aus Reiseführern und historischen Abrissen auf.

HG: Ist es der Wunsch, vieles zu wissen, oder Dinge, die auf Sie Eindruck machen, aufzuschreiben?

JMB: Naja, ursprünglich wollte ich die ganze Geschichte aufschreiben, aber das war zu mühsam, und so blieb es bei den Personen der Handlung.

HG: Sie sind also eine Art Register zu Enzyklopädien, die eben nicht existieren.

JMB: Mir gefallen die Namen einfach.

HG: Was ist denn ihre Thematik?

JMB (Pause): Könige, Helden und die Straße.

HG: Ihr Bild der Straße ist aber dadurch verschönert, daß Sie die Straße verschönern.

JMB: Ich glaube, ich muß diese Krone an Keith Haring weiterreichen. Ich habe seit langem nicht mehr auf der Straße gearbeitet.

HG: Und der Übergang von SAMO zu Jean Michel, war das ein Reifeprozeß?

JMB: SAMO habe ich mit einem Mitschüler gemacht. Ich wollte den Namen einfach nicht behalten.

HG: Aber er wurde Ihr Name...

JMB: Es war irgendwie ... ich war gewissermaßen der Architekt. Und es gab Techniker, die mit mir arbeiteten.

HG: Macht es Ihnen Spaß, in Europa auszustellen, und das ganze Verfahren – ein Händler lädt Sie ein, Sie fahren hin und schauen sich die Ausstellung an...

JMB: Meistens muß ich selbst hinfahren und muß auch mein Ticket bezahlen, weil ich nicht weiß, wie man auf diplomatische Art darum bittet...

HG: Sie sind auch ein wenig schroff.

JMB: Und dann will ich meistens mit Freunden hinfahren und muß auch für sie bezahlen.

HG: Am Ende also haben Sie wenig an der Ausstellung verdient.

JMB: Das macht nichts.

HG: Gefällt es Ihnen, dort zu sein, wo die Gemälde sind?

JMB: Meistens muß ich diesen Händlern auf die Finger schauen, ob sie die richtigen Arbeiten ausstellen. Oder einfach sicher gehen, daß sie es richtig machen.

HG: How about the transition from SAMO back to Jean Michel, was that growing up?

JMB: SAMO I did with a high school friend, I just didn't want to keep the name.

HG: But it became yours...

JMB: It was kind of like ... I was sort of the architect of it. And there were technicians who worked with me.

HG: Do you like showing in Europe and the whole enterprise of having a dealer invite you, going over and looking at the show...

JMB: Usually, I just have to go myself and I have to pay my own ticket 'cause I don't know how to ask diplomatically...

HG: You are a bit abrupt.

JMB: And then I usually want to go with friends so I have to pay for them as well.

HG: So you end up not making very much money out of your show.

JMB: It's okay.

HG: Do you like the idea of being where the paintings are?

JMB: Usually I have to check up on these dealers and make sure they're showing the right work. Or just make sure that it's right.

HG: I like the drawings that are just lists of things.

JMB: I was making one in an airplane once. I was copying some stuff out of a Roman sculpture book. This lady said, »Oh, what are you studying.« I said, »It's a drawing.«

HG: I think »What are you studying« is a very good question to ask – because your work does reflect an interest in all kinds of intellectual areas that go beyond the streets, and it's the combination of the two.

JMB: It's more of a name-dropping thing.

HG: It's better than that. You could say that about Twombly, and yet somehow he drops the name from within. With your work it isn't just a casual list. It has some internal cohesion with what you are.

JMB: My favorite Twombly is »Apollo and The Artist«, with the big »Apollo« written across it.

HG: When I first met you, you were part of the club scene ... the Mudd Club.

JMB: Yeah, I went there every night for two years. At that time I had no apartment, so I just used to go there to see what my prospects were.

HG: You used it like a bulletin board.

JMB: More like an answering service.

HG: *Ich mag die Zeichnungen, die aus Listen von Gegenständen bestehen.*

JMB: Ich habe einmal so etwas in einem Flugzeug gemacht. Ich zeichnete Sachen aus einem Buch römischer Skulpturen nach. Eine Dame fragte: »Oh, was studieren Sie da?« Ich sagte: »Es ist eine Zeichnung.«

HG: *Ich finde die Frage »Was studieren Sie da?« sehr berechtigt – denn Ihre Arbeit spiegelt tatsächlich ein Interesse für alle möglichen Geistesgebiete wider, die über die Straße hinausgehen, und stellt die Verbindung beider Sphären dar.*

JMB: Es ist eher »name dropping«.

HG: *Es ist mehr als das. Man könnte das über Twombly sagen, und doch läßt er den Namen von Innen herausfallen. Bei Ihrer Arbeit ist es nicht einfach eine zufällige Aufreihung. Da ist auch ein innerer Zusammenhang mit dem, was Sie sind.*

JMB: Mein Lieblings-Twombly ist »Apoll und der Künstler«, mit dem Namen »Apollo« in großer Schrift drüber.

HG: *Als ich Sie zum erstenmal kennenlernte, waren Sie ein Teil der Club-Szene ... im Mudd-Club.*

JMB: Ja, ich ging jeden Abend dorthin, zwei Jahre lang. Zu der Zeit hatte ich keine Wohnung, und so ging ich dorthin, um meine Chancen auszuloten.

HG: *Sie benutzten ihn wie ein Schwarzes Brett.*

JMB: Mehr wie einen Anrufbeantworter.

HG: *Sie haben vor einiger Zeit Ihr Telefon abgestellt. War das für Sie positiv?*

JMB: Ja, ziemlich. Jetzt kriege ich dauernd Telegramme. Es macht Spaß. Man weiß nie, was es sein könnte. »Sie werden zum Militär einberufen«, »Ich habe $ 2.000 für Sie«. Es könnte alles Mögliche sein. Und weil die Leute mit dem Telegramm mehr Geld ausgeben müssen, kommen sie gleich zur Sache. Aber jetzt klingelt es an meiner Tür auch mitten in der Nacht. Ich tue so, als wäre ich nicht zu Hause...

HG: *Wollen Sie ein Haus?*

JMB: Ich bin mir noch nicht im klaren darüber, welcher Teil der Erde nicht in die Luft gehen wird; ich weiß also nicht, wo ich es bauen soll.

HG: *Sie wollen also leben...*

JMB: Klar! Natürlich will ich leben.

HG: *Wollen Sie auf dem Land oder in der Stadt leben?*

JMB: Auf dem Land leide ich mehr unter Verfolgungswahn, wissen Sie? Ich finde, da draußen sind die verrückten Menschen noch ein bißchen verrückter.

HG: *You got rid of your telephone a while ago. Was that satisfying?*

JMB: Pretty much. Now I get all these telegrams. It's fun. You never know what it could be. »You're drafted,« »I have $2,000 for you.« It could be anything. And because people are spending more money with telegrams they get right to the point. But now my bell rings at all hours of the night. I pretend I'm not home...

HG: *Do you want a house?*

JMB: I haven't decided what part of the world isn't going to get blown-up so I don't know where to put it.

HG: *So you do want to live...*

JMB: Oh yeah, of course I want to live.

HG: *Do you want to live in the country or the city?*

JMB: The country makes me more paranoid, you know? I think the crazy people out there are a little crazier.

HG: *They are, but they also leave you alone more.*

JMB: I thought they'd be looking for you more, in the country. Like hunting, or something.

HG: *Have you ever slept in the country, over night?*

JMB: When I said I was never gonna go home again, I headed to Harriman State Park with two valises full of canned food...

HG: *In the summer?*

JMB: It was in the fall.

HG: *And you slept over night?*

JMB: Yeah, two or three days.

HG: *Were you scared?*

JMB: Not much. But yeah, in a way. You know, you see some guys with a big cooler full of beer. And it gets really dark in the woods, you don't know where you are.

HG: *Do you like museums?*

JMB: I think the Brooklyn is my favorite, but I never go much.

HG: *What did you draw as a kid, the usual stuff?*

JMB: I was a really lousy artist as a kid. Too abstract expressionist; or I'd draw a big ram's head, really messy. I'd never win painting contests. I remember losing to a guy who did a perfect spiderman.

HG: *But were you satisfied with your own work?*

JMB: No, not at all. I really wanted to be the best artist in the class, but my work had a really ugly edge to it.

HG: *Das sind sie, aber sie lassen einen auch eher in Ruhe.*

JMB: Ich dachte, sie würden einen mehr auflauern, auf dem Land. Wie auf der Jagd oder so.

HG: *Haben Sie jemals auf dem Land übernachtet?*

JMB: Als ich erklärte, ich würde niemals nach Hause zurückkehren, nahm ich Kurs auf Harriman State Park, mit zwei Koffern voller Konserven...

HG: *Im Sommer?*

JMB: Es war im Herbst.

HG: *Und Sie übernachteten dort?*

JMB: Ja, zwei oder drei Nächte.

HG: *Hatten Sie Angst?*

JMB: Nicht besonders. Und dann doch, auf gewisse Weise. Wissen Sie, man sah einige Jungs mit einer großen Kühltasche voll Bier. Und es wird im Wald richtig dunkel; man weiß gar nicht, wo man ist.

HG: *Mögen Sie Museen?*

JMB: Ich glaube, das Brooklyn Museum ist mir am liebsten, aber ich gehe nicht oft hin.

HG: *Was haben Sie als Kind gemalt, das übliche Zeug?*

JMB: Als Kind war ich wirklich ein schrecklicher Künstler. Zu abstrakt-expressionistisch. Oder ich zeichnete einen großen Bockskopf, richtig schlampig. Ich habe nie Malwettbewerbe gewonnen. Ich weiß noch, wie ich einem unterlag, der einen perfekten Spiderman machte.

HG: *Aber waren Sie selbst mit Ihrer Arbeit zufrieden?*

JMB: Nein, gar nicht. Ich wollte der beste der Klasse sein, wirklich, aber meine Arbeit hatte etwas richtig Häßliches an sich.

HG: *War das Zorn?*

JMB: Zu der Zeit gab es eine Menge häßlicher Szenen in meiner Familie.

HG: *Gibt es Zorn in Ihrer Arbeit heute?*

JMB: Sie besteht zu ungefähr 80% aus Zorn.

HG: *Aber es gibt auch Humor.*

JMB: Wenn man auf den Arsch fällt, lachen die Leute. Was ist denn das, Humor?

HG: *Was it anger?*

JMB: There was a lot of ugly stuff going on at the time in my family.

HG: *Is there anger in your work now?*

JMB: It's about 80% anger.

HG: *But there's also humor.*

JMB: People laugh when you fall on your ass. What's humor?

Dieses Gespräch erschien erstmals in: Interview Magazine, Januar 1983

Der verstorbene Henry Geldzahler war Kurator für Kunst des zwanzigsten Jahrhunderts am Metropolitan Museum of Art in New York und später Kunstbeauftragter der Stadt New York.

The late Henry Geldzahler was Curator of Twentieth Century Art at the Metropolitan Museum of Art in New York, and later was Commissioner of Art at the City of New York.

Jeffrey Hoffeld

Basquiat und der innere Mensch

Mit sieben Jahren wurde Jean Michel beim Spielen auf der Straße im New Yorker Stadtteil Brooklyn von einem Auto angefahren und schwer verletzt: seine Milz mußte herausoperiert werden. Wie bei vielen Künstlern, die gravierende Erkrankungen oder schwere Verletzungen in früher Kindheit überstanden, hat dieses lebensgefährliche Ereignis unauslöschliche Spuren in der Kunst Basquiats hinterlassen.

Während eines langen Krankenhausaufenthalts brachte seine Mutter ihm ein Exemplar von »Gray's Anatomy«, eine Faksimile-Ausgabe dieses berühmten britischen Einführungswerks zum Bau und zur Funktionsweise des menschlichen Körpers aus der Zeit der Jahrhundertwende samt detaillierten Stahlstichen. Darin war auch ein ausführlicher Abschnitt mit Text und Abbildungen über die Milz, ihre Entwicklung im Mutterleib, ihre Natur, Struktur und Funktion, die Lage der Milz im Gesamtzusammenhang der anderen lebenswichtigen Organe und deren chirurgische Behandlung im Krankheits- bzw. Verletzungsfall. Neben seinem spezifischen Interesse und seiner Neugierde in bezug auf die Natur der Milz konnte Jean Michel beim Durchblättern dieses Klassikers die ausführliche Darstellung der männlichen und weiblichen Sexualorgane mit zahlreichen begleitenden Abbildungen sowie die Bilder und Erläuterungen über die Entwicklung des Embryos und die Geburt nicht entgehen. In Basquiats Gemälden und Zeichnungen gibt es zahlreiche Beispiele seiner Verwendung anatomischer Bildmotive, die weitgehend auf dieses kostbare Geschenk der Mutter zurückgeht und später durch Studien weiterer Standardwerke auf diesem Gebiet, vor allem der wissenschaftlichen und medizinischen Traktate Leonardo da Vincis, vertieft wurde.

Durch diese entscheidenden Quellen angeregt, brachte Basquiat eine außerordentliche Vielfalt von Bildern hervor, die die Zerlegung und Untersuchung des menschlichen Körpers zum Thema haben. Zum einen stellt er isolierte Körperteile dar, die von erläuternden Beschriftungen begleitet werden, durchaus in der Darstellungweise der konventionellen medizinischen Lehrbücher. Zum anderen enthüllt er die inneren, organischen Prozesse seiner typischen Charaktere (darunter möglicherweise auch Selbstporträts), als ob wir, die Betrachter, mit einer besonderen röntgenähnlichen Sichtweise begabt wären, die uns befähigt, in den Körper eines Menschen hineinzublicken. Diese ungewöhnlichen Porträts des menschlichen Inneren scheinen einen metaphysischen Zweck zu haben: Während sie den Fleisch-und-Knochen-Aspekt des Menschseins betonen, erlauben sie uns, innerhalb der normalerweise verborgenen Bereiche des menschlichen Daseins die Suche nach der Seele aufzunehmen.

Keine umfassende Theorie kann die prominente Rolle der anatomischen Komponente in Basquiats Kunst ergrün-

Jeffrey Hoffeld

Basquiat and the inner self

At the age of seven, while playing on the streets of Brooklyn in New York City, Jean Michel was hit by a car. The resulting injuries required the removal of his spleen. As with many artists who survived grave illnesses or serious injury in early childhood, this life-threatening event left an indelible mark on Basquiat's art.

During his long hospital stay Jean Michel's mother brought him a copy of *Gray's Anatomy*, a facsimile edition, complete with detailed engravings, of the renowned turn-of-the-century British guide to the structure and workings of the human body, including a substantial section of text and illustrations about the spleen; its development during gestation; its character, structure, and functions; the position of the spleen with respect to other vital organs; and its surgical treatment in the event of disease or injury. Besides Jean Michel's specific concerns and curiosity about the nature of the spleen, flipping through the pages of this classic he could not have missed its extensive coverage of male and female sexual organs, accompanied by numbers of illustrations, as well as images and explanations pertaining to the development of the embryo and childbearing. There is abundant evidence in Basquiat's paintings and drawings of his use of anatomical imagery, informed, in large part, by this treasured gift from his mother, later enriched by his study of other mainstays in the field, especially Leonardo da Vinci's scientific and medical treatises.

Inspired by these crucial sources, Basquiat produced an extraordinary variety of images having to do with the dissection and examination of the human body. At times he represented isolated, individual body parts, shown disembodied from particular human specimens together with explanatory labels, much as they would be presented in conventional medical books. On other occasions the inner, organic workings of several of his stock characters (including what may be self-portraits) are revealed, as if we, as viewers have been equipped with special x-ray powers of observation, permitting us to peer inside people's bodies. These unusual portraits of the inner self appear to have a metaphysical purpose; while they emphasize the flesh and bones aspect of what it means to be human, they also enable us to soulsearch within the normally hidden regions of human existence.

No single, all encompassing theory can account for the prominence of this anatomical component of Basquiat's art. The complexity, frequency of appearance, and persistence of these representations suggest that their nearly obsessive use was motivated by more than just the artist's painful association of these images with his traumatic childhood experience. Basquiat's attachment to these images, especially skeletons, and their pictorial and iconographic significance for him can be better understood by examining them within the context of his predominant

den. Die Komplexität, Häufigkeit des Auftretens und Beharrlichkeit dieser Darstellungen sprechen dafür, daß die Motivation für ihre fast obsessive Verwendung durch mehr als bloß die schmerzliche Erinnerung des Künstlers an das traumatische Ereignis in seiner Kindheit zu erklären ist. Basquiats Vorliebe für diese Motive – besonders für Skelette – und ihre bildhafte und ikonographische Bedeutung für ihn kann man besser verstehen, wenn man sie im Zusammenhang mit seinen hauptsächlichen stilistischen Interessen sowie im Rahmen seiner erzählerischen Begabung mit ihren einfallsreichen narrativen Techniken betrachtet.

Sollte man Jean Michel im Krankenhaus damals, als er die wohl erste formelle Einführung in die Anatomie genoß, nicht darauf hingewiesen haben, so wird es ihm mit der Zeit offensichtlich geworden sein, daß das eingehende Studium des menschlichen Körpers in der grundlegenden Form des Skeletts zur Einsicht führt, daß die Hautfarbe, der Anlaß so vieler Streitigkeiten und so viel Elends bei den Schwarzen, eine ganz und gar oberflächliche Eigenschaft ist – nur so tief wie die Haut, wie man sagt –, die von der Universalität und Gleichheit anderer, bedeutsamerer gattungs- und geschlechtsspezifischen Charakteristika in Form und Funktion weit in den Schatten gestellt wird. Im Zusammenhang mit den vielen Aussagen und Metaphern über Rassenprobleme, die die Gemälde und Zeichnungen Basquiats bevölkern, zwingen uns diese anatomischen Zergliederungen und Schemata geradezu, das innere Wesen der Schwarzen zu betrachten, indem sie ihre Menschlichkeit herauskehren und ihre physische und seelische Verletzlichkeit offenbaren.

In stilistischer Hinsicht verbindet sich Basquiats wiederholte Verwendung anatomischer Motive – Skelette, Muskulatur, innerer Organe – mit der noch stärkeren Tendenz in seiner Arbeit, alles umzustülpen, die Innenseite nach außen zu kehren. Innere Gedanken treten in graffiti-artigen Litaneien aus Worten und anderen, explosionsartigen Ausrucksformen vor die Augen der Öffentlichkeit; die Grenzen zwischen der Privatsphäre und dem öffentlichen Bereich verschwimmen; Vergangenheit und Gegenwart werden miteinander vermischt, Realitätsebenen vervielfältigt und durcheinandergewürfelt; die imaginären Bereiche Paradies, Hölle und Fegefeuer werden ununterscheidbar. Basquiats Verschränkung des Inneren mit dem Äußeren erhält in einigen Gemälden eine reelle Dimension, wo er gewissermaßen das Knochengerüst der dem Gemälde zugrunde liegenden Skelettstruktur sichtbar macht, indem er die normalerweise abgeschnittenen und verborgenen Rahmenleisten oder Leinwandstützen von den vier Ecken am Bildrand herausragen läßt, wodurch ein gänzlich unkonventioneller Einblick in die inneren Zusammenhänge des Malerhandwerks zustandekommt und die »Gegenständlichkeit« des betreffenden Werks zusätzlich betont wird.

Die Segmentierung und Darstellung von Körperteilen in Basquiats Werk ist zudem ein Ausdruck seiner Vorliebe für die Fragmentierung als eine umfassende Methode der

stylistic concerns, as well as within the framework of his gifted storytelling and inventive narrative techniques.

If it was not pointed out to Jean Michel at the time of his convalescense when he probably received his first formal introduction to anatomy, then it would have eventually become obvious to him on his own that the study of the structure of the human body, seen in its most fundamental skeletal form, demonstrates that skin color, the cause of so much struggle and grief for black people is an altogether superficial trait – only skin deep, as it were, overshadowed by the universality and sameness of other more significant species-specific and gender-specific characteristics of form and function. Among the many messages and metaphors having to do with race that are embedded in Basquiat's paintings and drawings these anatomical dissections and diagrams, in particular, compel us to consider the inner beings of black people, reinforcing their humanity, making public their physical and spiritual vulnerability.

In stylistic terms Basquiat's repeated use of anatomical imagery – skeletons, musculature, and internal organs – coincides with an even more widespread tendency in his work to turn things inside out. Inner thoughts are made public in graffiti-like litanies of words and other bursts of expression; distinctions between private spaces and public places are dissolved; past and present are interwoven, and levels of reality are multiplied and scrambled; the imagined realms of paradise, hell, and purgatory become indistinguishable. Basquiat's commingling of inside and outside takes on a literal dimension in several paintings in which he chose to expose the bare bones, as it were, of the painting's underlying, skeletal structure by extending the normally concealed and mitered stretcher bars or canvas supports beyond each of the four corners of the picture's edge, providing an entirely unconventional insight into the inner workings of the painter's craft, and further emphasizing the »objectness« of the work in question.

The segmentation and display of body parts in Basquiat's work is also one manifestation of his preference for fragmentation as a more general mode of picture-making, storytelling, and as a way of treating materials. He seems to have been driven to pull things apart, examine their inner workings, consider the harmony or discord of their parts, and to reassemble them in some semblance, however elaborate the artifice of reordering, of wholeness. He imposed this vision on storytelling, as well as on the human figure. In his use of materials he devised similar means of deconstruction and reassembly, as in his use of separate, often unrelated sheets of drawings as collage elements on canvas, forming intricate hieroglyphic patterns of words and pictures, which challenge the viewer to stitch together, from loosely related shards and fragments, a reading of the whole.

There is another possible explanation for the recurrent use of anatomical, especially skeletal, imagery in Basquiat's

Bildkomposition, des Erzählens einer Geschichte und der Behandlung von Material. Es scheint, als hätte er die Dinge erst auseinanderreißen müssen, um dann ihre Funktionsweise, die Harmonie bzw. den Mißklang ihrer Teile – je nachdem – festzustellen, wonach er sie wieder zu irgendeinem Anschein von Ganzheit zusammenstellte, und sei der Kunstgriff dieser wiederhergestellten Ordnung noch so ausgefallen. Er zwang diese Sicht der menschlichen Gestalt ebenso auf wie dem Geschichtenerzählen. In der Verwendung von Material dachte er sich ähnliche Methoden der Dekonstruktion und Neuzusammenstellung aus, beispielsweise in der Verwendung von eigenständigen, oft gar nicht zum Thema passenden Zeichnungsblättern als auf Leinwand montierte Collage-Elemente, die verwickelte Hieroglyphenmuster aus Worten und Bildmotiven bilden, die den Betrachter herausfordern, aus den Scherben und Fragmenten eine Lesung des Ganzen zusammenzuflicken.

Die wiederholte Verwendung anatomischer und vor allem Skelettmotive in Basquiats Gemälden und Zeichnungen kann noch eine Erklärung haben, die mit einem bekannten Aspekt des Lebens des Künstlers in Einklang zu bringen ist: mit seinen Drogenerfahrungen. Basquiat ist ja im Alter von 27 Jahren an einer Überdosis gestorben. Die durch Kokain oder Heroin ausgelösten körperlichen Gefühle waren ihm durchaus vertraut. Er kannte auch literarische Darstellungen der qualvollen Erfahrung der Drogenabhängigkeit und der Entziehung, vor allem aus der Feder der »Beat«-Generation.

Basquiat kannte den Beat-Lyriker Allen Ginsberg persönlich; er las die Werke Jack Kerouacs; vor allem war er mit William Burroughs freundschaftlich verbunden. Basquiat zitierte in seinen Werken Passagen aus Burroughs' Kultbuch »Junky«, in dem der Autor, der Ich-Erzähler des Buches, über seine eigene Drogenabhängigkeit berichtete, und mindestens einmal haben die beiden gemeinsam Drogen eingenommen.

In »Junky« beschreibt Burroughs die Qual, die er und andere durch die Drogenabhängigkeit sowie durch den Versuch durchmachten, von den Opiaten loszukommen. Seine lebendige Schilderung des gequälten Junky-Daseins enthält viele Details der körperlichen Marter des Drogensüchtigen, wie sie in den inneren Organen, der Muskulatur, dem Knochengerüst verspürt werden – all das wird in Basquiats intensiver Beschäftigung mit den inneren Vorgängen des menschlichen Körpers auf ganz ähnliche Weise in den Vordergrund gestellt. Burroughs beschreibt die Schwierigkeit, sich überhaupt zusammenzuhalten, während »der Organismus drauf und dran war, sich in seine Einzelteile aufzulösen.« »Morphium befällt« – nach Burroughs' Darstellung – »zuerst die Rückseite der Beine, dann den Nacken: eine sich ausbreitende Welle der Entspannung, die die Muskeln derart von den Knochen löst, daß man ohne Konturen zu schweben scheint, wie wenn man im warmen Meerwasser liegt.« Mit dem Einsetzen extremer Übelkeit geht – wie man in »Junky« nachlesen

paintings and drawings that is consistent with what we know about one aspect of the artist's life, his involvement with drugs. Basquiat died at the age of twenty-seven from a drug overdose. The physical sensations associated with the abuse of cocaine and heroin were well known to him. He was also familiar with literary accounts, especially in the writings of the Beat Generation, of agonizing experience linked to addiction and withdrawal.

Basquiat socialized with the poet Allen Ginsberg, he read the work of Jack Kerouac, and he became especially friendly with William Burroughs. Basquiat made word references in his work to Burrough's cult book *Junky*, the author's first-person account of his own drug addiction, and, on at least one occasion, the two used drugs together.

In *Junky*, Burroughs describes the anguish he and others experienced from addiction, as well as from attempts to withdraw from the use of opiates. His vivid portrait of the pained existence of the junky contains many references to the physical torment of the addict, experienced in the internal organs, musculature, and bone structure – all of which is similarly emphasized in Basquiat's preoccupation with the inner workings of the human body. Burroughs describes the difficulty of holding oneself together as the »organism was always on the point of disintegrating into its component parts.« »Morphine«, as Burroughs describes it, »hits the back of the legs first, then the back of the neck, a spreading wave of relaxation slackening the muscles away from the bones so that you seem to float without outlines, like lying in warm salt water.« As feelings of extreme sickness set in they are accompanied, as we read in *Junky*, by the sensation of »subsiding into a pile of bones.«

The special, often exalted place of body parts and dissections in Basquiat's work, resonant of ex voto plaques and their evocation of healing prayers, also suggests that there is a ritual or ceremonial purpose to these works. Unlike the more clinical approach to the representation of human anatomy found in standard medical texts, including *Gray's Anatomy*, there is a consistently provocative, often haunting, liturgical quality to Basquiat's use of his imagery. This aspect of Basquiat's iconography has prompted some writers to suggest that there is a voodooistic intent in his art. Although he was familiar with a variety of occult practices and religious beliefs (including voodoo), outside the Judeo-Christian traditions, specific evidence of these practices within Basquiat's work are difficult to isolate. While there are certainly signs of a rich mixture of African-American, Puerto-Rican, and Haitian religious influences in Basquiat's art, their precise nature and meaning have not, as yet, been convincingly charted, suggesting fertile ground for further study of the artist's belief systems, his investigation of other cultures, and the place of these interests in his work.

Although there are cults, as Basquiat was probably aware, that require prospective priests and shamans to con-

kann – eine Empfindung einher, »als wäre man nur mehr ein Haufen Knochen.«

Der besondere, oft hervorgehobene Stellenwert von Körperteilen und Seziertem in Basquiats Œuvre, die an Ex-voto-Plaketten mit ihren implizierten Appellen um Heilung erinnern, legt den Schluß nahe, daß diese Werke auch eine rituelle oder zeremonielle Funktion haben. Anders als der klinische Ansatz zur Darstellung der menschlichen Anatomie, die in den medizinischen Standardwerken, darunter »Gray's Anatomy«, zu finden sind, hat Basquiats Verwendung dieser Motive eine konsequent provokative, oft betörend-liturgische Qualität, aufgrund deren manche Kritiker einen Voodoo-Aspekt in Basquiats Kunst konstatiert haben. Obwohl er eine ganze Anzahl okkulter Praktiken und religiöser Vorstellungen außerhalb der gängigeren aus der jüdisch-christlichen Tradition kannte (darunter auch Voodoo), fällt es schwer, spezifische Zeugnisse dieser Praktiken in Basquiats Werk dingfest zu machen. Gewiß sind Anzeichen einer reichen Vielfalt religiöser Einflüsse afroamerikanischer, puertoricanischer und haitischer Prägung in Basquiats Kunst festzustellen, aber ihre genaue Beschaffenheit und Bedeutung sind bis dato nicht auf überzeugende Weise ergründet worden; hier ist ein fruchtbares Feld für weitere Untersuchungen der Glaubenssysteme des Künstlers und ihrer Rolle in seinem Werk.

Obwohl manche Kulte, wie Basquiat vermutlich bekannt war, angehenden Priestern bzw. Schamanen vorschreiben, sie müßten als eine von vielen Initiationsübungen vor mystischen Unternehmungen oder um die Ekstase zu erreichen ihr eigenes Skelett betrachten, kann die wiederholte Verwendung von Skeletten bei Basquiat nicht ohne weiteres einer gezielten Absicht zugeschrieben werden. Andererseits bestätigt unsere Erfahrung, daß diese Elemente in seinem Werk oft befremdend und verunsichernd auf uns wirken. Das unablässige Hervorbringen angstgetriebener, kämpferischer, konfrontationsfreudiger Gestalten, die frenetische Energie seiner weitschweifigen Texte, die Quantität und Vielfalt der gruseligen Todesmetaphorik in der Kunst Basquiats sind Äußerungen der Seelenqual des Künstlers. Der Tod und die Betrachtung der eigenen Sterblichkeit haben sich schon in jungen Jahren als feste, wohl unerbittliche Koordinaten im Bewußtsein Basquiats etabliert, aus denen ein chronischer Sinn für das Verhängnisvolle entstand, dem sich weder er noch seine Kunst entziehen konnte.

Sommer und Herbst 1998
New York City

Jeffrey Hoffeld ist Schriftsteller in New York.

template their own skeletons as one of the many initiatory exercises preceding mystical undertakings or the attainment of ecstasy, Basquiat's repeated use of skeletons is not easily attributable, as we have seen, to a single-minded purpose. We do, however, know that our experience of these elements in his work is often disturbing and unsettling. The unrelenting outpouring of anxiety-ridden, struggling figures; the frenetic energy of his garrulous texts; and the quantity and diversity of chilling metaphors for death in Basquiat's art are harrowing manifestations of the artist's own tormented psyche and inner being. Death and the contemplation of one's own mortality were established, early on, as fixed, apparently unforgiving coordinates in Basquiat's consciousness, engendering a chronic sense of doom from which he and his art could not escape.

Summer and Fall 1998
New York City

Jeffrey Hoffeld is a writer living in New York City.

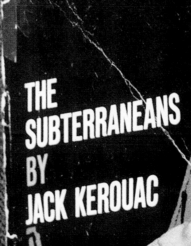

Jeffrey Hoffeld

Basquiat und die Unterirdischen

*Er [Basquiat] konnte alles und jedes verwenden und
bewundern, wenn er meinte, er könnte dadurch etwas
lernen. Und entgegen aller Erwartung, unter dem Anschein (oder sollte man eher Schutz sagen?) eines
»schwierigen Charakters«, einer Haltung aus Scheu und
außerordentlichem Stolz zugleich, nahm er es auf wie an
einer wunden Stelle, als ginge ihm alles, womit er in
Berührung kam, wirklich und oft schmerzlich nahe.*

Francesco Pellizzi

Werbefotos für die letzte New Yorker Ausstellung seines
Lebens zeigen Basquiat mit einem zerlesenen Exemplar
von Jack Kerouacs Roman »The Subterraneans« (»Die
Unterirdischen«) in Händen. Basquiat war zwar mit William Burroughs und Allen Ginsberg (den bekanntesten
überlebenden Schriftstellern der »Beat«-Generation, die
beide enge Beziehungen zur New Yorker Kunstszene
unterhielten) persönlich befreundet, aber Kerouac, der
1969 mit 47 Jahren an einer Blutung im Unterleib als Folge des Alkoholismus gestorben ist, gehörte nicht zu seinen literarischen Bekanntschaften. Dem jungen Künstler
werden jedoch genug Aspekte im Werk Kerouacs aufgefallen sein, die zur eigenen Kunst und zu seinem Leben
Bezug hatten, wodurch ersichtlich wird, weshalb er sich
in den letzten Monaten seines tragischen Lebens an diesem schmalen Band so festhielt.

Es ist nicht klar, inwieweit Basquiat die sonstigen Schrif-
ten Kerouacs kannte oder ob ihm Details aus dem Leben
und Umfeld des Schriftstellers bekannt waren. Wußte er
beispielsweise, daß Kerouac, der als Jean-Louis Lebris de
Kerouac geboren wurde, Französisch-Kanadier war und
daß seine erste Sprache das Joual (der dortige Dialekt des
Französischen) und nicht Englisch war? Wußte Basquiat,
daß Kerouac als Kind um Akzeptanz und Eingliederung in
die amerikanische Kultur kämpfen mußte? Hat er auch
Kerouacs »Visions of Gerard« gelesen? Hätte ihn dieser
Roman, in dem der Autor (der den in der Familie üblichen
Kosenamen Ti Jean führt) die allzu kurze Geschichte seines älteren Bruders erzählt, der mit neun Jahren am
rheumatischen Fieber starb, etwa deshalb angesprochen,
weil sein eigener Vater Gerard hieß? Wußte Basquiat,
dessen Milz nach einem Unfall im Kindesalter entfernt
werden mußte, daß Kerouacs Vater als junger Mann an
Milzkrebs gestorben ist? Wenn Basquiat diese Dinge
gewußt hätte, hätte ihm jeder dieser starken Aspekte im
Leben des Schriftstellers durch ihre offensichtlichen Par-
allelen zu seiner eigenen Erfahrung wie von selbst den
Stoff zu einer tiefen Beziehung zu Kerouac als Seelenbru-
der geliefert.

»The Subterraneans«, wie Kerouac im ersten Absatz des
Buches berichtet, ist »die Geschichte eines un-selbstbe-
wußten und gleichzeitig egomanen Mannes«, der die
Gelegenheit zu einer aus seiner Sicht lebenslangen Nähe

Jeffrey Hoffeld

Basquiat and the subterraneans

*He (Basquiat) could use and marvel at anything he
thought he could learn from. And, rather unexpectedly,
under the guise (or should one say protection?) of a
»difficult character«, a disposition both shy and singular
proud, there was a raw receptivity, as if all he came into
contact with really touched him, often painfully.*

Francesco Pellizzi

Publicity shots for the last New York show of his life-
time picture Basquiat clutching a dog-eared copy of Jack
Kerouac's novel *The Subterraneans*. Although Basquiat
knew William Burroughs and Allen Ginsberg (the most
prominent surviving members of the Beat Generation of
writers, both of whom maintained close ties to the New
York art world), Kerouac, who died at the age of forty-
seven in nineteensixtynine of abdominal hemorrhaging
brought on by alcoholism, was not one of his literary
acquaintances. However, the young artist very likely saw
enough in Kerouac's work that related to his own art and
life to explain a tight grip he had on this slim volume in the
final months of his tragic life.

To what extent Basquiat was familiar with Kerouac's other
writings, or aware of any of the details of the writer's life
and times is unclear. Did he know, for example, that
Kerouac, born Jean-Louis Lebris de Kerouac, was French
Canadian, and that his first language was joual, not
English? Was Basquiat aware of Kerouac's childhood
struggles with acceptance and assimilation into American
culture? Did he also read Kerouac's *Visions of Gerard?*
Would he have been attracted, because of his father's
name – Gerard, to his novel, in which the author (identified
by his family's name for him – Ti Jean) tells the abbrevia-
ted life story of his older brother who died at the age of
nine from rheumatic fever?

Did Basquiat, whose spleen had to be removed when
he was little because he was hit by a car, know that
Kerouac's father died of cancer of the spleen when he was
a young man?

Where they known to Basquiat, each of these powerful
ingredients in the writer's life, with their obvious parallels
in the painter's own experience, would have provided the
makings for a compelling relationship with Kerouac as
soul-mate to the young artist.

The Subterraneans, as Kerouac informs us in the book's
opening paragraph, is »the story of an unself-confident
man, at the same time an egomaniac«, who throws away
what may well be, as he sees it, the opportunity of a life-
time for loving closeness with a woman. Leo Percepied
(whose name may have something to do with shooting
oneself in the foot), the first-person narrator of the novel,
admits that he has no one but himself to blame for the
outcome. Percepied, a white writer, falls in love with Mar-

zu einer ihn liebenden Frau wegwirft. Leo Percepied (dessen Name möglicherweise mit dem Sich-selbst-in-den-Fuß-Schießen zusammenhängen soll), der Ich-Erzähler des Romans, gibt zu, daß er das Ergebnis nur sich selbst vorzuwerfen hat. Percepied, ein weißer Schriftsteller, verliebt sich in Mardou Fox, die teils indianischer, teils schwarzer Abstammung ist: »die schwarze Mutter tot anläßlich ihrer Geburt – der unbekannte Halbblut-Cherokee-Vater Landstreicher«. Ganz im Zeichen der offenen, einfühlsamen Haltung der Beat-Schriftsteller der schwarzen urbanen Kultur Amerikas gegenüber ist Kerouac für die Nuancen ihrer gemischtrassischen Beziehung im durchaus zur Gewalt bereiten rassistischen Umfeld aufgeschlossen. Er weiß beispielsweise, daß Mardou sich nie mit Leo Händchen haltend in der Öffentlichkeit zeigen würde, weil sie befürchtet, die Menschen auf der Straße würden sie dann für eine bloße Nutte ansehen.

Bei der ersten Begegnung ist Leo überhaupt nicht sicher, daß er sich mit ihr weiter einlassen will. Er ist überzeugt, daß Mardou ihn nicht mögen werde und seine guten Seiten und Stärken nicht sehen könne, die »schon lange ersoffen« sind, wie er erzählt, »unter jahrelangem Drogenkonsum und dem Wunsch zu sterben, aufzugeben, alles aufzugeben und zu vergessen, im dunklen Stern zu sterben.« Und höchstwahrscheinlich um sich selbst zu schützen, ist er, je näher er mit Mardou in Beziehung kommt, über ihre rassische Andersartigkeit zunehmend besorgt, und seine Kenntnis von ihrem früheren Wahnsinn beschäftigt ihn anhaltend, denn er sorgt sich, daß, weil »sie richtig verrückt gewesen war«, es leicht noch einmal passieren könnte. Leo hat den Wahnsinn selbst kennengelernt, der teilweise durch Drogen und Alkohol herbeigeführt worden war, und seine Haltung dazu ist ernüchternd: »Wie klar erkennt man es, wenn man wahnsinnig wird – das Denken verstummt, in der Physis passiert gar nichts, Urin sammelt sich in den Lenden, die Rippen ziehen sich zusammen.«

Leos kleinliche Eifersüchteleien, sein Verfolgungswahn, unbewußter Rassismus und vor allem seine quälenden Selbstzweifel vergiften schließlich die Beziehung. Am Ende wird die traurige Mär ihrer Auseinandersetzungen und des Auseinandergehens in Leos »Buch der Tränen«, wie er es nennt, aufgezeichnet: »The Subterraneans«. Der Roman endet damit, daß Leo nach Hause zurückkehrt, nachdem er Mardou verloren hat, um die Geschichte ihrer unglücklichen Beziehung zu schreiben. Sie beginnt mit seiner Einschätzung der Gründe, warum die Sache schief gelaufen ist: Wie er die Unabhängigkeitserklärungen Mardous sowie »ihre Abneigung gegen jegliche Bindung« nicht beachtet hatte; wie er sich trotz dieser Warnungen auf sie stürzte, als wollte er sich wehtun, sich selbst »Schnittwunden zufügen« – »noch einen Schnitt dazu und sie ziehen mir das blaue Gras 'rüber und lassen den Kasten 'runterplumpsen – Mann!« Obwohl wir über Leos Zukunft am Schluß noch im unklaren sind, glaubt er selbst, sein Tod sei sehr nahe, er breite seine »großen Flügel über mei-

dou Fox, who is part American Indian and part black, »Negro mother dead for birth of her-unknown Cherokee-halfbreed father a hobo«. Characteristic of the open, sympathetic attitude of the Beats toward America's urban black culture, Kerouac is sensitive to the nuances of their interracial relationship in a potentially violent racist environment. He knows, for example, that Mardou won't hold hands with Leo in public because she's afraid that people on the street will think she's just a hustler.

When they first meet, Leo is not at all sure that he wants to get involved. He's convinced that Mardou won't like him and that he can't see his good points and virtues, »long been drowned«, as he tells us, »under years of drugtaking and desiring to die, to give up, to give it all up and forget it all, to die in the dark star«.And, in all likelihood, defensively, as he gets closer to Mardou, he is increasingly concerned about their racial differences, and he dwells on what he knows of Mardou's former madness, worrying that because »she'd been seriously insane«, it could very well happen again. Leo has known madness himself, induced, in part, by drugs and alcohol, and he has a chilling take on it: »How clear the realization one is going mad – the mind has a silence, nothing happens in the physique, urine gathers in your loins, your ribs contract.«

Leo's petty jealousies, paranoia, unwitting racism, and, above all, his excruciating self-doubt eventually poison their relationship. In the end, the mournful tale of their struggles and breakup is recorded in Leo's »tearbook«, as he calls it, The Subterraneans. The novel ends with Leo returning home, after losing Mardou, to write the story of their ill-fated affair. It begins with his assessment of what went wrong: how he didn't listen to Mardou's declarations of independence, »her distaste for involvement«, and how he hurled himself at her, in spite of these warnings, as if he wanted to be hurt, to »lacerate« himself – »one more laceration yet and they`ll pull the blue sod in, and make my box plop boy.« Although, as the book closes, we are uncertain of Leo's future, he believes his death is very near, bending »big wings over my window … I see it, I hear it, I smell it, I see it in the limp hang of my shirts destined to be not worn, new-old, stylish-out-of-date, neckties snake-like behung I don`t even use anymore, new blankets for autumn peace beds now writhing rushing cots on the sea of self-murder…«

Kerouac's confessional novel, like the most of his voluminous writing, barely conceals the real-life experiences of its actual author. Ann Charters, Kerouac's biographer and editor of a volume of his letters, says he wrote The Subterraneans in a »three day and three night Benzedrine-fueled burst« at his mother's kitchen table in Queens, following the breakup of his own love affair, kept secret from his family, with a young black woman. Although the story itself is set in San Francisco, it is, in fact, about the underground and after hours life of New York's East Village. »The Subterraneans« is actually the name Allen Ginsberg gave to his circle of Beat Generation friends, which, of

nem Fenster aus … ich sehe ihn, ich höre ihn, ich rieche ihn; ich erkenne ihn daran, wie meine Hemden schlaff dahängen, dazu bestimmt, nicht getragen zu werden, neu-alt, modisch-überholt, Krawatten schlangenartig verknäult, die ich überhaupt nicht mehr trage, neue Decken für herbstlichen Frieden, Betten, jetzt sich windend, hurtig, Pritschen auf dem Meer des Selbstmords –«

In Kerouacs Bekenntnisroman, wie so oft in seinem volu-minösen Werk, sind die tatsächlichen Lebenserfahrungen des Autors kaum verhüllt. Ann Charters, Kerouacs Bio-graphin und Herausgeberin eines Bandes seiner Briefe, sagt, er habe »The Subterraneans« »in einem von Benze-drine angetriebenen Wurf von drei Tagen und drei Näch-ten« am Küchentisch seiner Mutter in Queens geschrie-ben, nachdem eine Liebesbeziehung zu einer jungen Schwarzen, die er seiner Familie verheimlicht hatte, zu Ende gegangen war. Die Story spielt zwar in San Francisco, sie handelt aber in Wirklichkeit vom »unterirdischen« Nachtleben im »East Village« von New York. »The Sub-terraneans« ist eigentlich der Name, den Allen Ginsberg seinem Freundeskreis aus der Beat-Generation gab, zu dem natürlich auch Jack Kerouac gehörte. Wer im Bilde war, als das Buch 1958 herauskam, hätte wohl die fiktiven Namen den jeweiligen wirklichen Personen mühelos zu-ordnen können. Aber Kerouac, der weite Strecken seines Lebens bei seiner Mutter wohnte, wollte nicht, daß dieser Aspekt seines Daseins seiner Familie bekannt werde. Er hat die tatsächlichen Charaktere und den Spielplatz auch wohl deshalb leicht verschleiert, um einer möglichen ge-richtlichen Untersuchung zuvorzukommen, eingedenk der aufsehenerregenden Sittlichkeitsklage in San Francisco gegen Ginsbergs »Howl and Other Poems« im Jahre 1957.

Wie im Werk Basquiats nehmen der Jazz und eine Reihe von Jazz-Größen, vor allem Charlie Parker, in »The Subter-raneans« sowohl stilistisch als auch inhaltlich einen bedeu-tenden Platz ein. Da ist Leos Augenzeugenbeschreibung eines Auftritts von »Bird«, wie er sich »mit seinem Publi-kum identifizierte … und Mardou und mir in der Kindheit unserer Liebe zusah.« In seinem Aufsatz »Brushes with Beatitude« (abgedruckt im Katalog der Basquiat-Retro-spektive im Whitney-Museum im Jahre 1992) weist Klaus Kertess auf das Foto des Jahres 1988 hin, in dem Basqui-at den Roman Kerouacs in der Hand hält, und während er lediglich bemerkt, daß der Roman durch seinen Inhalt Bas-quiat angesprochen habe, weil er die Geschichte eines gemischtrassischen Paares erzählt, geht Kertess auf den Stil des Romans, die Beziehung zum Jazz und die Ver-wandtschaft, die Basquiat im Entstehungsprozeß bei Kerouac entdecken sollte, nicht näher ein. Wie schon Ker-tess feststellt, hat Kerouac versucht, »seinen Stil mit dem improvisierten Fluß des Jazz zu durchdringen«. Basquiat hat wohl starke Ähnlichkeiten im »unentwegten Wechsel der Verbalzeit, der Person und des Gesichtspunkts« im Roman, »im Kontrapunkt des Erzählflusses mit dem emphatischen Rhythmus der tönenden Worte« mit sei-nem eigenen Ideal der Spontaneität und freier Assoziation

course, included Jack Kerouac. Those in the know at the time the book was published in 1958 could probably have easily matched up the fictional names of the characters with their real-life counterparts. However, Kerouac, who lived with his mother for much of his life, did not wish to reveal this part of his existence to his family. He may also have thinly veiled the actual players, as well as their loca-le, in response to potential legal exposure suggested by the highly publicized obscenity case in San Francisco invol-ving Ginsberg's *Howl and Other Poems* in 1957.

As in Basquiat's work, jazz and a number of jazz greats, especially Charlie Parker, have a significant place in both the style in which *The Subterraneans* was written and its story-line, including Leo's first-hand account of Bird in per-formance »digging his audience… watching Mardou and me in the infancy of our love.« Klaus Kertess, in his essay »Brushes with Beatitude« (which appears among the essays by several writers in the Whitney Museum's Bas-quiat retrospective catalogue, published in 1992) remarked in the 1988 photograph of Basquiat holding Kerouac's novel, and while, in terms of the book's content, he mere-ly referred to the appeal it was likely to have for Basquiat because of its treatment of a racially mixed couple, Ker-tess did not comment or examin the style of the novel, its connections to jazz, and the kinship Basquiat would disco-ver in Kerouac's writing process. As Kertess points out, Kerouac attempted to »imbue his writing with the extem-poraneous flow of jazz.« Basquiat would have seen strong resemblances in the novel's »run-on changes of tense, person, and place, its counterpointing of narrative flow with the emphatic rhythms of the sounded words« to his own commitment to spontaneity and free association, resulting in the torrential outpouring of words, images, scrawls, and flourishes of color in his paintings, drawings, and constructions.

Kerouac credited jazz with being the principal source of his distinctive stylistic inventions. His »wild form«, »sketching language«, and »spontaneous prose«, terms he used to describe the characteristics of his prose, were all deriv-ed, as he tells us, from observing the performances of Lester Young, Charlie Parker, Charlie Mingus, and others. He discovered in their music a rhythm of language he wanted to make his own. As Ann Charters has observed, »Trying to capture the emotional truth of his direct expe-rience, Kerouac let the words pour out onto the page instead of editing them in the writing process.« And his direct inspiration for this writing style, no doubt obvious to Basquiat, was the improvisatory style of the jazz musician. Writing about his techniques, Kerouac defined his »sket-ching language« as the »undisturbed flow from the mind of personal secret idea-words, *blowing* (as per jazz musici-an) on subject of image.«

Just as Basquiat could readily recognize and respond to the style of *The Subterraneans* (and perhaps, had been directly influenced by it at an earlier point in his artistic development) as well as the subculture of its Beat night-

erkannt, die in einem überbordenden Erguß von Worten, Bildern, Kritzeleien und schwungvoll hingeworfener Farbe in seinen Gemälden, Zeichnungen und Konstruktionen seinen Ausdruck findet.

Kerouac sagte selbst, der Jazz sei die Hauptquelle seiner eigenen stilistischen Erfindungen gewesen. Seine »wilde Form«, »skizzierende Sprache« und »spontane Prosa« – so beschrieb er selbst die Eigenart seiner Prosa – seien alle nach seiner Darstellung aus der Beobachtung von Auftritten von Lester Young, Charlie Parker, Charlie Mingus und anderen geschöpft. In ihrer Musik hat er einen Sprachrhythmus entdeckt, den er sich zu eigen machen wollte. Wie Ann Charters bemerkt hat, »ließ Kerouac, indem er die gefühlsmäßige Wahrheit des unmittelbar Erlebten einzufangen suchte, die Worte aufs Papier hinfließen, anstatt sie im Schreibprozeß zu redigieren.« Und seine unmittelbare Inspiration für diesen Schreibstil, wie Basquiat kaum entgangen sein kann, war der improvisierende Stil des Jazzmusikers. In bezug auf seine Schreibtechnik definierte Kerouac seine »skizzierende Sprache« als »den ungestörten Gedankenfluß der persönlichen, geheimen Idee-Worte, ein Blasen (in der Art eines Jazzmusikers) über das Thema ›Bild‹.«

So wie Basquiat der Stil von »The Subterraneans« sowie die Subkultur des Beat-Nachtlebens in Bars und anderen Schuppen sofort angesprochen und ihm verwandt erscheinen mußte (und er vielleicht in einem früheren Stadium seiner künstlerischen Entwicklung durch das Buch unmittelbar beeinflußt worden ist), hat er sich gewiß in der Beschreibung im Roman vom »Teerauchen«, »Highwerden« und den Saufgelagen wie auch im aufgeladenen Geisteszustand des Autors beim Schreiben wiedererkannt. Durch seinen Kontakt zu Burroughs (dessen Kultbuch »Junky« in Basquiats Werk ausdrücklich genannt wird) und die wohlbekannte Tatsache des Drogenkonsums der Beat-Schriftsteller wird Basquiat der Stellenwert von Drogen als Mittel zur Flucht aus einer fremden Welt und, wie Klaus Kertess bemerkt, als »Umsetzungsmittel beim künstlerischen Schaffen« vertraut gewesen sein.

In »The Subterraneans« hat Basquiat wohl auch die Bedeutung entdeckt , die man dem Sex als Mittel zur Flucht und Zugang zur Kreativität beigemessen hat. Im Gegensatz zu den Versuchen der »redenden Klasse« (wie die materialistische Kultur im Roman einmal apostrophiert wird), die Erfahrung rational zu erklären und abstrakte Paradigmata aufzustellen, stellt Percepied »Die Funktion des Orgasmus« des Wilhelm Reich als endgültiges Modell der Klarheit hin. Wir wissen nicht, ob Basquiat Reichs Werk schon kannte, obwohl auch hier einiges dafür spricht, daß Verweise auf Reichs »orgone box« bei ihm auf Verständnis gestoßen wären. Auf jeden Fall hätte er unter den »Unterirdischen« eine besondere Aufgeschlossenheit für die Ideen Reichs gefunden. Ein Freund Leos baut in der Tat einen Orgone-Akkumulator, um damit seine eigene sexuelle Heilung zu suchen, und als Mardou einmal beim

life in bars and other hangouts, he would certainly have easily identified with the novel's many accounts of »smoking tea,« »getting high,« and heavy drinking, including the obviously hyper-charged state of its author when he was writing this book. From his contact with Burroughs (whose cult book *Junky* is actually named in Basquiat's work) and the widespread knowledge of the Beat's involvement with drugs, Basquiat would have known the value given to drugs as a means of escape from an alien world, and, as Klaus Kertess observes, as a mode of »transport into the making of art.«

In *The Subterraneans* Basquiat would also have found evidence of the value given to sex as a means of escape and transport to creativity. In contrast to the attempts of the »Talking Class« (as materialist culture ist referred to at one point in the novel) to rationalize experience and to offer abstract paradigms, Percepied offers Wilhelm Reich's *The Function of the Orgasm* as the ultimate model of clarity. We do not know whether Basquiat already knew Reich's work, although there is, once again, reason to believe that talk of Reich's »orgone box« would have been familiar to him. Nonetheless, he would have found among the subterraneans a special affection for Reich's ideas. One of Leo's friends actually builds an orgone accumulator in order to undertake his own sexual healing, and Mardou, immersed on one occasion in Leo's sex with her, is described as »lost« in it, experiencing »Reich's beclouding of the senses.« Writing about the ideal mental state in which to create, Kerouac prescribed writing »without consciousness« in »semitrance,« »excitedly, swiftly ... in accordance ... with laws of orgasm ... Reich's ›beclouding of consciousness.‹ *Come* from within out – to relaxed and said.«

Of course, the pursuit of sex for Kerouac, as may very well have been the case for Basquiat, is inextricably tied up with a crying need for tenderness and loving closeness. Yet, as we know, Leo (the barely disguised Ti Jean), and, perhaps Jean Michel, too, was not easily given to surrendering himself to what he needed most: »I'd put my face close to hers (Mardou's) to talk about books, she'd turned her face to me close, it was an ocean of melting things and drowning, I could have swimmed in it, I was afraid of all that richness and looked away...« And it was Mardou who saw through the situation, declaring to Leo that »Men are so crazy, they want the essence, the woman is the essence, there it is right in their hands but they rush off erecting abstract constructions.«

It comes as no surprise, given Kerouac's own strong attachment to his mother, thal Leo's love for Mardou and his grave sense of loss about their ended affair are somehow entangled with his feelings about his mother. She comes to him in his time of bereavement in a vision of extraordinary tenderness and caring that must have been painfully stirring reading for Basquiat, whose mother, as reported in Warhol's *Diaries,* had been »in and out of men-

Sex mit Leo völlig aufgeht, wird sie als »weggetreten« beschrieben: Sie erlebt »Reichs Benebelung der Sinne«. Bezüglich des idealen Geisteszustands für den Schaffensprozeß fordert Kerouac das Schreiben »ohne Bewußtsein«, im »Halbtrancezustand«, »aufgeregt, schnell … nach … den Gesetzen des Orgasmus … Reichs ›Benebelung des Bewußtseins‹. Kommen von innen nach außen – nach entspannt, gesagt.«

Natürlich war für Kerouac, wie auch durchaus im Falle Basquiats, die Suche nach Sex mit dem gesteigerten Bedürfnis nach Zärtlichkeit und liebevoller Nähe untrennbar verbunden. Und doch, wie wir wissen, fiel es Leo (dem kaum getarnten Ti-Jean) und vielleicht auch Jean Michel nicht leicht, sich dem hinzugeben, was er am meisten brauchte. »Ich war mal mit dem Gesicht ganz nahe an das ihre [Mardous], um über Bücher zu reden, sie wandte das ihre ganz nahe an meines, es war ein Meer zerfließender Dinge, ein Ertrinken, ich hätte darin schwimmen können, ich hatte Angst vor all der Fülle und schaute weg …« Und es ist Mardou, die die Situation durchschaut, als sie Leo sagt, »Die Männer sind so verrückt, sie wollen das Wesentliche; die Frau ist das Wesentliche, da ist es, regelrecht mit Händen zu greifen, aber sie laufen weg und bauen sich abstrakte Gebäude.«

Es ist nicht verwunderlich, angesichts der starken Bindung Kerouacs zur Mutter, daß Leos Liebe zu Mardou und sein tiefes Gefühl des Verlustes, als die Beziehung zu Ende ist, irgendwie mit seinen Gefühlen zu seiner Mutter verstrickt sind. Sie kommt zu ihm in der Zeit seines Verlustes in einer Vision von außerordentlicher Zärtlichkeit und Zuwendung, die für Basquiat eine schmerzlich-spannende Lektüre gewesen sein muß, denn seine Mutter war, wie Warhols Tagebücher berichten, »mal in psychiatrischen Anstalten, mal wieder draußen« gewesen und war dem leidenden jungen Künstler emotional oder auch nur als physische Präsenz nicht verfügbar:

»… Ich sah das Gesicht meiner Mutter zu mir heruntergebeugt … eine Vision der Liebe meiner Mutter zu mir – jenes ausdruckslose und zwar deshalb so ausdruckslos weil so verständnisvolle Gesicht, zu mir heruntergebeugt in der Vision meines Schlafes, und mit Lippen, die nicht so sehr zusammengepreßt als beharrlich waren, als wollten sie sagen ›Pauvre Ti Leo, pauvre Ti Leo, tu souffri, les hommes souffri tout, y'ainque toi dans le monde j'va't prendre soin, j'aim'ra beaucoup t'prendre soin tous tes jours mon ange‹ – ›Armer kleiner Leo, armer kleiner Leo, du leidest, alle Menschen leiden, du bist ganz allein auf der Welt, ich werde dich umsorgen, ich wollte dich gern dein Leben lang umsorgen, mein Engel‹.«

New York, Juli - August 1998

tal hospitals,« unavailable to the suffering young artist, emotionally and physically:

»…I saw bending over the visage of my mother … a vision of my mother's love for me – that expressionless and expressionless-because-so-profound face bending over me in the vision of my sleep, and with lips not so pressed together as enduring and as if to say »Pauvre Ti Leo, pauvre Ti Leo, tu souffri, les hommes souffri tout, y'ainque toi dans le monde j'va't prendre soin, j'aim'ra beaucoup t'prendre soin tous les jours mon ange.« – »Poor Little Leo, poor Little Leo, you suffer, men suffer so, you're all alone in the world I'll take care of you, I would very much like to take care of you all your days my angel.«

New York City, July - August 1998

Jeffrey Deitch

Jean Michel Basquiat
Eine Hommage

Für viele von uns, die wir im unteren Manhattan vor neun, zehn Jahren lebten, spielte Jean Michel Basquiat eine Rolle, noch bevor wir ihn kennenlernten oder wußten, wer er denn sei. Als Straßenpoet Samo schienen seine beunruhigenden Sprüche, eine Art surreale Verkehrung der Werbeslogans, und seine unverkennbare Unterschrift überall präsent zu sein. Diese mysteriöse Persönlichkeit hinterließ sein einprägsames Zeichen bei jedem neuen Club, auf der Mauer jedes Gebäudes, wo interessante Kunst zu sehen war oder wo interessante Menschen wohnten.

Jean Michel hatte bereits eine so unverkennbare Sichtweise, eine so sichere Hand, selbst als Teenager, daß er nur einige Züge mit einem Lackstift an der Mauer zu machen brauchte, um diese Bilder, und wenn sie noch so spärlich ausgeführt waren, unvergeßlich zu machen, und dennoch waren sie in der ihm eigenen Art gemacht. Es gibt sehr wenige Künstler, die eine so kraftvolle Persönlichkeit haben, daß sie ihre ganze Ästhetik durch das Ausführen weniger Züge zum Ausdruck bringen können.

Lernte man dann Jean Michel kennen, so verstand man, warum seine Linie und Unterschrift so kraftvoll waren. Er war eine Persönlichkeit wie keine andere – erstaunlich vielseitig, intelligent, leidenschaftlich, teilnehmend, großzügig. Er war ein Mann von solcher Ausstrahlung und Charakterstärke, daß nur ein Blick, einige kurze Worte, ein paar Linien auf dem Papier sehr viel mitteilen konnten.

Jean Michel hat es fertiggebracht, bis zum zwanzigsten Lebensjahr das Gros der Kunstgeschichte intuitiv in sich aufzunehmen. Die ersten Werke, die er öffentlich ausstellte, machten Furore und wurden sofort mit denen großer moderner Künstler verglichen. Aber Jean Michels Aussage war sein ureigenes Eigentum. Er erfand ein Vokabular, einen Sinn für Komposition, eine neue Art, das Medium der Malerei einzusetzen, um die Intensität und das Durcheinander der heutigen urbanen Wirklichkeit einzufangen. Er faßte zusammen, was im Fernsehen, in den Galerien, auf den Straßen zu sehen war, indem er die Sprachen der modernen Kunst und jener, die ihr vorausgegangen war, durcheinanderwarf, um zu einer umfassenden zeitgenössischen Sichtweise zu gelangen.

Jean Michel war Künstler im weitesten Sinne – nicht bloß ein großer Maler, sondern auch ein großer Poet. Natürlich kein Poet nach der stereotypen romantischen Art – aus dessen Feder Verse über sanfte Hügel und romantische Träumereien fließen. Er stellte ein markantes Porträt des Bewußtseins unserer Zeit dar. Ich glaube, daß in Zukunft die literarischen Qualitäten von Jean Michels Werk ebenso bewundert werden wie die visuellen. Ich weiß von keinem modernen Künstler, dem es gelungen ist, das Verbale und Visuelle so schlagend zu verbinden.

Jeffrey Deitch

Jean Michel Basquiat
An Homage

For many of us who lived downtown about 9–10 years ago, Jean Michel Basquiat was already a presence in our lives before we had ever met him or even knew who he was. As the street poet Samo, his unsettling phrases, a kind of surreal version of advertising slogans, and his distinctive signature seemed to be everywhere. This secret person left his unforgettable mark outside every new club, on the walls of every building where interesting art could be seen, or where especially interesting people were living.

Jean Michel already had such a distinctive vision, such a sure hand, even as a teenager, that he could just draw a few lines or make a few marks on the wall with a Magic Marker, and these images, however spare, were unforgettable, and they were uniquely his. There are very few artists who had such a force of personality, who could express their whole aesthetic just by drawing a few lines.

When you met Jean Michel you understood why that line and signature were so powerful. He was a personality unlike any other - a remarkable breadth, intelligence, passion, sympathy, generosity. He was a person with such charisma and strength of character that just his look, a few terse comments, a few lines drawn on paper, could communicate so much.

Somehow Jean Michel had managed to intuitively absorb most of modern art history before he was twenty. His first publicly exhibited works caused a sensation and were immediately compared to those of some of the great modern artists. But Jean Michel's statement was uniquely his own. He invented a vocabulary, a sense of composition, a new way to use the medium of painting that captured the intensity and the disjointed quality of today's urban reality. Jean Michel's statement summed up what was happening on TV, in the galleries, and on the streets, churning the languages of modern and pre-modern art to encompass a totally contemporary vision.

Jean Michel was an artist in the broadest sense – not just a great painter, but a great poet. Not, of course, a poet in the stereotyped romantic mode – penning verse about rolling hills and romantic reveries, but presenting an arresting portrait of contemporary consciousness. In the future, I think that the literary qualities of Jean Michel's work will be admired as much as the visual qualities. I don't know of any modern artist who has merged the verbal and the visual so effectively.

Jean Michel accomplished enough in ten years to earn a place as one of the great artists of our time. It is perhaps a little strange to describe a person who many of us in the art world knew so well in elevated, historical terms. But Jean Michel really was a genious – someone with truly

Jean Michel hat in zehn Jahren so viel erreicht, daß er zu den großen Künstlern unserer Zeit gezählt wird. Es wirkt vielleicht ein wenig seltsam, jemanden, den viele von uns in der Kunstszene so gut gekannt haben, mit so erhabenen historischen Begriffen zu versehen. Aber Jean Michel war tatsächlich ein Genie – jemand mit wirklich bemerkenswerten Eigenschaften auf allen Ebenen. Ich werde sein erstaunliches Gedächtnis nie vergessen. Mich konnte er damit frappieren, daß ihm eine kleine Bemerkung, die ich vier Jahre zuvor gemacht hatte, noch immer präsent war.

Jean Michel war ein ungewöhnlicher Mensch, nicht nur wegen seines Talents und seiner Leistungen: Er war auch eine bemerkenswerte Persönlichkeit, jemand, der sich selbst immer treu blieb – der stets darum kämpfte, daß man ihn nicht übervorteilte. Ein Mann mit der nötigen Willenskraft, um sich durchsetzen zu können, um andere dazu zu bringen, das Spiel nach seinen Regeln zu spielen. Und in ihren Gesprächen der letzten Monate haben die Freunde Jean Michels alle über seine unglaubliche Großzügigkeit gestaunt. In einer Zeit, in der der traditionelle Künstlerbrauch, eigene Werke anderen zu schenken, im Schwinden begriffen ist, hat Jean Michel Dutzende – wenn nicht Hunderte – seiner eigenen Werke verschenkt.

Andy Warhol erzählte mir, wie er Jean Michel vor Jahren kennengelernt hat, als er ungefähr fünfzehn war. Jean Michel verkaufte damals bedruckte T-Shirts in Greenwich Village und ging zu Warhols Atelier, um Geld für Malermaterialien zu borgen. Andy gab ihm vielleicht $ 25, damit er verschwinde. Als Jean Michel etwa fünf Jahre später begann, etwas Geld zu verdienen, ging er wieder Andy besuchen, um ihm das Geld zurückzugeben.

Jean Michel legte der Welt gegenüber eine aggressive Haltung an den Tag, gleichzeitig war er mit Freunden ungewöhnlich warmherzig und großzügig. Wir werden uns lange an sein gewinnendes, fast unschuldiges Lächeln und seinen Humor erinnern, den er oft gegen die Galeristen einsetzte, die ihn übervorteilen wollten. Im vergangenen Frühjahr erzählte er mir, wie er einen Kunsthändler, den er unnötig knauserig fand, dazu brachte, seine enorme Zeche und die seines Freundes in einem Nobellokal zu übernehmen.

In einer Zeit, in der die Kunst fast so etwas wie ein Beruf – wie der eines Anwalts oder so – geworden ist, wo die Künstler versuchen, die richtigen Schulen zu besuchen und die richtigen Leute zu beschwatzen, ist Jean Michel seinen eigenen Weg gegangen. Er hat es so gemacht, wie er es für richtig hielt, nicht wie es andere tun. Er wird für andere eine bleibende Inspiration sein, ein Beweis, daß, egal wo ein Künstler beginnt, er durch die Kraft seiner Persönlichkeit und durch Fleiß die Aufmerksamkeit der Welt gewinnen und mit Tausenden wetteifern kann.

Viele von uns haben intensive Erinnerungen an ihn und werden ihn schwer vermissen. Aber Jean Michel hat nicht nur Erinnerungen hinterlassen, sondern auch eine Legende. Ich bin sicher, daß die Menschen in hundert Jahren und sogar danach vor seinem Werk staunend verweilen werden.

remarkable qualities on all levels. I'll never forget his remarkable memory. He could astonish me by recalling off-hand comments that I had made four years before.

Jean Michel was an extraordinary person not only for his remarkable talent and accomplishments: he was a remarkable personality as well. He was someone who was always his own man – who was always fighting to keep people taking advantage of him. Someone with the force of will to get his own way, to play the game his way. And talking with friends of Jean Michel over the last few months, we have all marvelled over his incredible generosity. In a time when the traditional artist's custom of giving artwork as gifts has diminished, Jean Michel gave away dozens if not hundreds of his works.

Andy Warhol told me a story about first getting to know Jean Michel years ago, when he was about fifteen. Jean Michel was selling printed T-shirts in Greenwich Village and went up to Andy Warhol's studio to try to borrow money to buy materials. Andy gave him about $ 25 to get him to go away. One of the first things that Jean Michel did when he started to make some money about 5 years later was to go visit Andy to pay him back.

Jean Michel took a tough stance toward the world, but at the same time was uncommonly warm and generous with his friends. We will long remember his engaging, almost innocent smile and his sense of humor, which was often directed at art dealers who were trying to take advantage of him. Last spring he described to me how an art dealer whom he found unnecessarily cheap, was manipulated into picking up an enormous check for Jean Michel and his friend in a fancy restaurant.

In an era when art is becoming almost a profession - like being a lawyer – when artists try to go to the right schools, try to chat up the right people – Jean Michel took his own path. He did it his way, not someone else's way. He will long be an inspiration to people, a demonstration that no matter where an artist starts, by force of personality and application, one can capture the attention of the world and rival thousands.

Many of us have very strong memories and will miss him badly. But in Jean Michel's case, it's more than memories that will live on. He has left behind not just memories but a legend. I am sure that 100 years from now and even beyond, people will still be astounded by his work.

The above text was the eulogy to Jean Michel Basquiat at his funeral in 1988.

Diesen Text trug Jeffrey Deitch bei der Trauerfeier für Jean Michel Basquiat im Jahre 1988 vor.

A. R. Penck, Jean Michel Basquiat, 1996 Acryl auf Leinwand 70 x 50 cm

A.R. Penck

Poem for Basquiat

I say to you hello
the struggle against the past
would be tomorrow
with x-ray eyes
    through the stone-walls
    through the mountains of flesh
    through the brain-projections
        self-infections
    through all the books of mathematics
            physics
            politics
a b c
      ex
        way
          said
tomorrow without sorrow
      the beat
        crazy
      the drive
        lazy
such life
        down-town
kill the clown
        hit
come on begin
to drive to the sources of the dark river
        clever
nevermore for ever
        drive in
dangerous for the liver
deeper than the bottom of the sea
higher than high
  grasp the beaver

open the box with the mad key
true with that lie
false with that truth
to wit. to win. to draw
a new artificial law
you can't loose
bite the lion through the neck
invisible dreck
check out the possibilities
        of the creative field
without debt. without guilt
      fucking tiger
      fucking river
      fucking jungle
      fucking boat
        a gallery
be careful baby
what means automatism
  after the night
break the fascism
the original cataclysm
  the big splash
  the hard crash
    be tide
only with feeling
  the last thing
    without a cry
I say to you goodbye

Dublin 1984

aus: Katalog. Jean Michel Basquiat,
Mary Boone Gallery, New York 1984
mit freundlicher Genehmigung des Künstlers

Für Jean Michel

du:
schön und undurchschaubar wie eine frau
ich ziehe die schichten deines
schwarzen schönes gesichts ab
auf der suche nach jener stelle
kleiner blinder liebe
wo du freudig miles davis
und jack kerouac über den weg liefst.
coke heroin und haschisch
mindern nicht den glanz
der verführung, ungehindert
blendet er deine seele
wie verzweifelt berechnest du
namen und farben
sie flechten ein gewebe aus lügen
das unbesiegbar ist
du versuchst es.

Francesco Clemente
New York, 13. Juli 1998

---

aus: Katalog Jean Michel Basquiat, Témoignage 1977–1988,
Galerie Jérôme de Noirmont, Paris 1998
mit freundlicher Genehmigung des Künstlers

For Jean Michel

you:
handsome and secretive like a woman
i peel the layers of your
black beautiful face
searching for that place
of little blind love
where you met in joy miles davis
and jack kerouac.
coke heroin and grass
cannot dull your shine of
seduction, unhindered it
blinds your soul
frantic you compute
the names and colors
they weave a web of lies
which cannot be defeated
you try.

Francesco Clemente
New York, July 13, 1998

Francesco Clemente, Jean Michel Basquiat, ca. 1984   Aquarell auf Papier

Jean Michel Basquiat, Francesco Clemente, 1985 Öl auf Leinwand

Francesco Clemente

Für Diego

Afrika liegt dem Mittelmeer näher als New York, und für mich waren die schwarzen Amerikaner schon immer die Römer der Neuen Welt. Ihre literarische Stimme, von den zwanziger Jahren bis heute, ist Ausdruck eines klassischen Sinns für Maß und Menschlichkeit. Sie hat mit der Avantgarde des zwanzigsten Jahrhunderts – hektisch, minimalistisch, von der Maschine inspiriert – nichts zu tun. Langsam, stoisch und cool, hat die afroamerikanische literarische Stimme die übertriebene Klarheit, das Wohlwollen von jemandem, der zu einem taubstummen Kind spricht.

Jean Michel Basquiat teilte mit dieser Tradition einer sanften Menschlichkeit eine Sehnsucht nach einer anthropomorphen Form der Schönheit, die Eloquenz und Ruhe ausstrahlt. Das Format seiner Gemälde war nie zu groß, immer die Länge eines Arms. Die Schrift war nie verdreht im gotischen Graffitigeflecht. Jean Michels Worte sind mit der Geduld und Entschlossenheit eines Lehrers hingeschrieben, der seinen Schülern die Anfangsgründe der Schrift beibringt. Auf gleiche Weise trug Jean Michel die Farbe nach einem cartesischen Raster auf, streng waage- und senkrecht, als Metapher der Rationalität.

In der Mode der Alten Welt untadelig gekleidet, bestand Jeans einziges Zugeständnis an das Tempo der heutigen Mode in seinen Turnschuhen. Die High-Tech-Sohlen von Nike sind in vielen seiner Bilder zu sehen. Aber so kostspielig man sich auch einkleidet, als junger Schwarzer in der Stadt muß man natürlich immer imstande sein, sich im Laufschritt davonzumachen.

Jeans letzte Ausstellungsreklame zeigt ihn mit Jack Kerouacs »Subterraneans« unterm Arm. In den Gedichten Kerouacs tritt Charlie Parker als ein wohlwollender Buddha auf, der den gequälten Dichter beruhigt: »Es wird alles gut«. Für Jean war es beruhigend und eine Art Legitimation, sich als Erbe von Charlie Parker, Thelonious Monk, Coltrane und Miles anzusehen. In den Gemälden Jean Michels strahlen die Farben völlig unbefangen, sie »beißen« sich mit schockierender Objektivität; dabei realisieren sie Charlie Parkers zen-ähnliche Anweisung: »Spiel' die schönen Töne und spiel' sauber«.

Jean Michels Krone hat drei Zacken, nach seinem dreifachen königlichen Geblüt: Dichter, Musiker und großer Boxmeister. Großartige Boxer sind den Malern am ähnlichsten. Jean forderte alles heraus, was ihm stark vorkam, egal von welchem Geschmack oder Alter es war. (...). Jean erinnert sich an uns alle, ein wahrhafter Star, der aus den Wolken, in einem sich selbst verwischenden Hollywood/afrikanischen Paradies, auf uns sein Lebewohl herunterlacht!

New York, 1996

Francesco Clemente

For Diego

Africa is closer to the Mediterranean than to New York, and I have always seen black Americans as the Romans of the New World. Their literary voice, from the twenties until today, seems to express a classical sense of measure and humanity. It does not partake in the XX century avant-garde, frantic, minimalist, machine inspired. Slow, stoic and cool, the African American literary voice has the exaggerated clarity, the goodwill of someone who is talking to a deaf child.

Jean Michel Basquiat shared with this tradition of gentle humanism a longing for an anthropomorphic form of beauty, eloquent and calm. The format of his paintings was never too large, always arm's length. The writing was never twisted in the gothic lace of graffiti. Jean Michel's words are spelled with the patience and determination of a teacher who is showing his pupils the rudiments of writing. In the same way Jean Michel calmly applied the paint along a Cartesian grid, strictly horizontal and vertical, a metaphor for rationality.

Impeccably clad in old world clothes Jean's only concession to the speed of contemporary fashion was his sneakers. Nike's high-tech soles are liberally printed on many canvases. But of course no matter how expensive your attire is, if you are black and young in the city you should always be ready to run.

Jean's last exhibition ad shows him holding, under his arm, Jack Kerouac's »Subterraneans«. In Kerouac's poetry Charlie Parker appears as benevolent Buddha, spelling »all is well« to the tormented poet. Jean felt reassured and legitimized by the great lineage of Charlie Parker, Thelonious Monk, Coltrane and Miles. On Jean Michel's paintings, colors resonate without apology, clash with one another with shocking objectivity. They realize visually Charlie Parker's Zen-like instruction: »play the pretty notes and play clean«.

Jean Michel's crown has three peaks, for his three royal lineage: the poet, the musician and the great boxing champion. Boxing champions are the most similar to painters. Jean measured his skill against all he deemed strong, without prejudice as to their taste or age. (...) Jean remembers us all, a true star laughing from clouds above, in self-erasing Hollywood African paradise, farewell!

New York, 1996

aus: Jean Michel Basquiat, Témoignage 1977–1988
Galerie Jérôme de Noirmont, Paris 1988
mit freundlicher Genehmigung des Künstlers

Katalog

Catalogue

Papa, I will be very, very famous one day.

Papa, ich werde eines Tages sehr, sehr berühmt sein.

He's twenty-two years old, he's black and he's part of history.
Henry Geldzahler, 1981

Er ist zweiundzwanzig Jahre alt, er ist schwarz und er ist Teil der Geschichte.
Henry Geldzahler, 1981

Untitled (Car crash), 1980   Acrylic, spray paint, marker and varnish on canvas   101.5 x 75.5 cm

Masque, 1982   Oil on canvas   142 x 125 cm

Red Kings, 1981   Acrylic and oil paint sticks on wood and glass window   81 x 93.5 cm

My subject matters are royalty, heroism, and the streets. 1985
Meine Themen sind Könige, Helden und die Straßen. 1985

obscured makes you want to read them. 1984

Ich streiche Worte durch, damit Du sie besser sehen kannst: Dadurch,
daß sie verdeckt sind, möchtest Du sie lesen. 1984

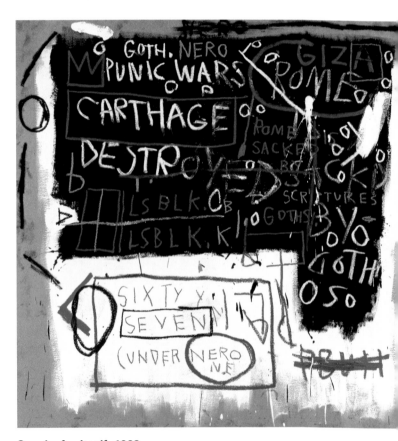

Speaks for Itself, 1982
Triptych, acrylic and oilstick on pressboard
122 x 122 cm each panel

I don't know how to describe my work because it's not always the same thing. It's like asking Miles Davis, well, how does your horn sound?

Ich weiß nicht, wie ich mein Werk beschreiben soll, weil es nicht immer dasselbe ist. Es ist so, als ob man Miles Davis fragen würde: »Nun, wie klingt Deine Trompete?«

Untitled (Tar And Feathers), 1982   Acrylic, oil, tar, feathers on wood   274 x 236 cm

Jersey Joe Walcott, 1982   Acrylic and oilstick on canvas and exposed wood support   183 x 183 cm

Hannibal, 1982   Acrylic, oilstick and paper collage on canvas   152.5 x 152.5 cm

Defensive Orange, Offensive Orange, 1982   Acrylic, oilstick and paper collage on wood   183 x 244 cm

Untitled, 1981   Acrylic and crayon on wood   58.5 x 62 cm

**I don't even know if I want to be called a black painter,
I just want to be me. Y'know. 1982**
Ich weiß nicht einmal, ob ich ein schwarzer Maler genannt werden
möchte, ich möchte nur ich sein, wissen Sie. 1982

Venus, 1982 Oilstick on canvas 12.5 x 10 cm

Fake, 1983   Oil and acrylic on canvas   214 x 214 cm

Franz Kline ist einer meiner Favoriten, aber ich wollte
Karikaturist sein. 1983

New, 1983 Oil and acrylic on canvas 214 x 214 cm

**Franz Kline is one of my favorites, but I wanted to be a
cartoonist. 1983**

Side View of An Oxen's Jaw, 1982 Acrylic on canvas 160 x 150 cm

Untitled, 1984   Collage and acrylic on canvas   109 x 109 cm

Arteries of the Left Arm, 1983   Oil, crayon, collage on canvas   160 x 150 cm

A next, 1984   Acrylic, colored oilstick, glue, colored xerox and wood collage on panel   101.5 x 138 x 11 cm

…siebzehn war, tr… …avon, ein Star zu sein. …ich dachte an all meine Helden, Charlie Parker, Jimi Hendrix.... Ich hatte eine romantische Vorstellung davon, wie Leute berühmt geworden sind.

Blue Heads, 1983
Acrylic and oilstick on hinged canvas   183 x 234 cm

Untitled 1981   Oil, oilstick and spray paint on canvas   130.2 x 142.9 cm

Old Cars, 1981   Acrylic, oilstick and paper collage on canvas   122 x 120.3 cm

Zuchero Mixed media on canvas 30.5 x 23 cm

I was writing gold on all that stuff and I made all this money right afterwards. 1987

Ich schrieb »Gold« auf all diese Dinge und verdiente daraufhin all dieses Geld. 1987

Su Azucar   Mixed media on canvas   30.5 x 23 cm

I just want to live life like James Dean.

Ich möchte nur das Leben leben wie James Dean.

Untitled (Bicyclist), c. 1984 Mixed media (oil on canvas) 203 x 269 cm

Untitled (Picasso Poster), undated   Acrylic painted Picasso Exhibition Poster   71 x 49 cm

Boone   Paper collage, felt tip pen and colored oil
stick on masonite, mounted on panel   104 x 30.5 cm

Maood, 1985   Acrylic and oil on wood   126 x 91.5 cm

Mr. Kipper, 1983   Acrylic and colored oilstick on canvas   183 x 142 cm

Untitled (Half Moon), 1985 Acrylic and oil on wood   229 x 112 cm

Untitled, 1985 Oil, acrylic, colored xerox collage and nails on wood 135 x 64 cm

Blue Skies, 1985   Acrylic and mixed media on wood   70 x 210 cm

Cash Crop, 1984 Oil and acrylic on canvas 183 x 244 cm

Flexicon, 1986 Acrylic, oil and collage on wood   198 x 91.5 cm

Untitled (Dodge Coupé), 1986   Acrylic on canvas   150 x 150 cm

Untitled, 1987   Acrylic and oilstick on canvas   188 x 238.5 cm

Untitled (Ober), 1986 Acrylic on canvas 150 x 119.5 cm

Embittered, 1986   Collage, pencil and painting on wood   126 x 184 cm

Untitled (Fist), 1986   Oil and coffee on canvas   80 x 60 cm

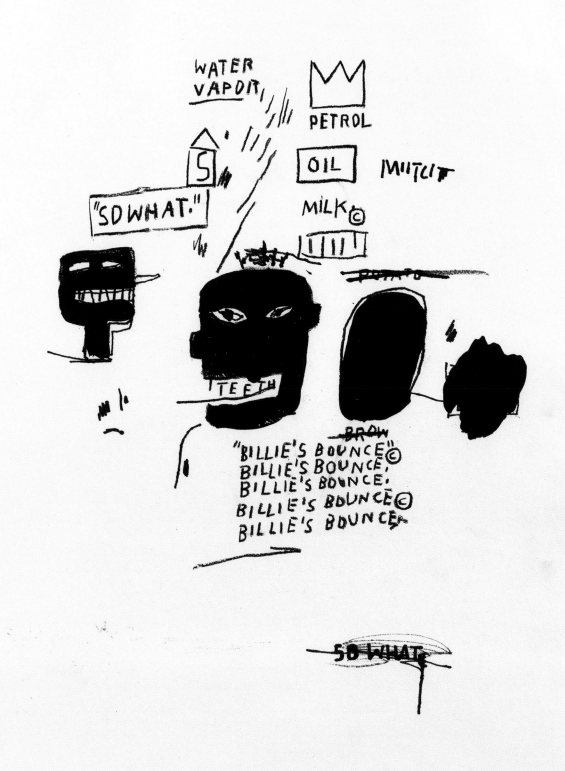

Untitled (Billie's Bounce), 1983   Oilstick on paper   80 x 59.5 cm

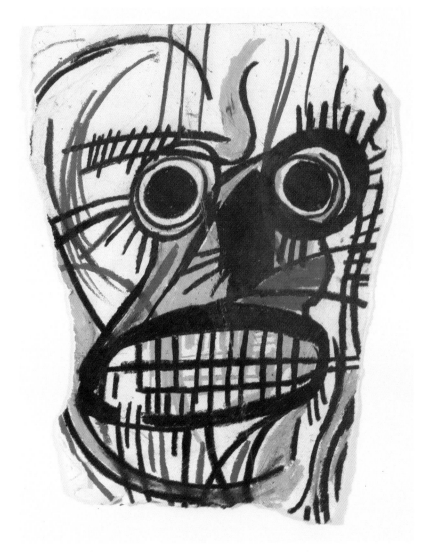

Untitled (Skull), 1982   Oil stick on paper   21.5 x 16.5 cm

Untitled, 1982   Oilstick on paper   52.5 x 39.5 cm

Procession, 1986   Acrylic and wood relief on wood   162 x 244 cm

**Picasso arrived at primitive art in order to give of its nobility
to western art. And I arrived at Picasso to give his nobility to
the art called »primitive«.**
Picasso kam zur primitiven Kunst, um ihre Noblesse der abend-
ländischen Kunst hinzuzufügen; ich kam zu Picasso, um seine
Noblesse jener Kunst zu geben, die man »primitiv« nennt.

Untitled (Lung), 1986   Acrylic on wood   244 x 140 cm

Life Like Son of Barney Hill, 1983
Six panels hinged together – acrylic, oilstick and xerox collage on canvas with metal hinges   122 x 522 cm

Untitled (Portrait), 1984   Oil stick and colored pencil on paper   76 x 56.5 cm

Untitled (Andy Warhol), 1984   Oilstick on paper   56.5 x 76 cm

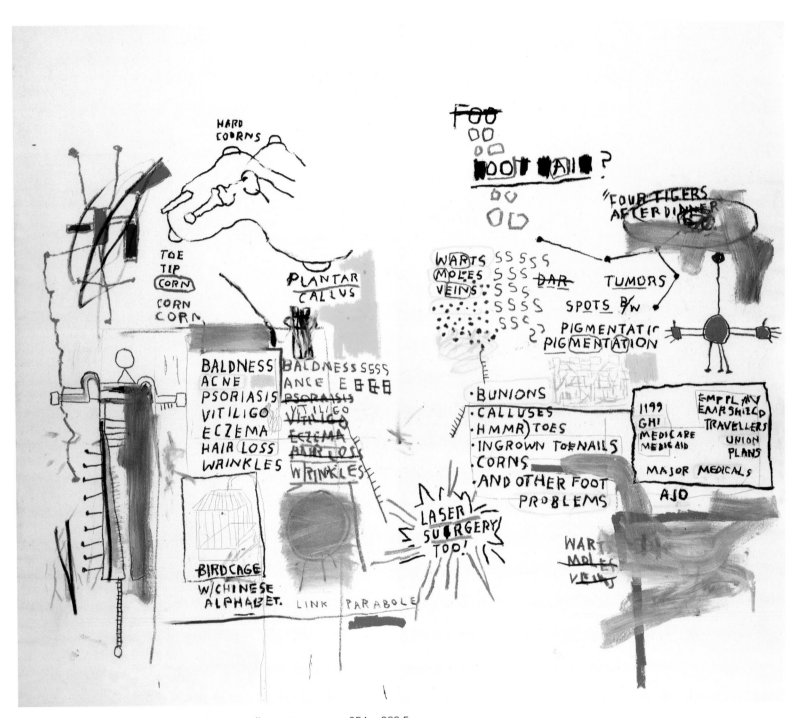

Untitled, 1988   Acrylic, oilstick and xerox collage on canvas   254 x 288.5 cm

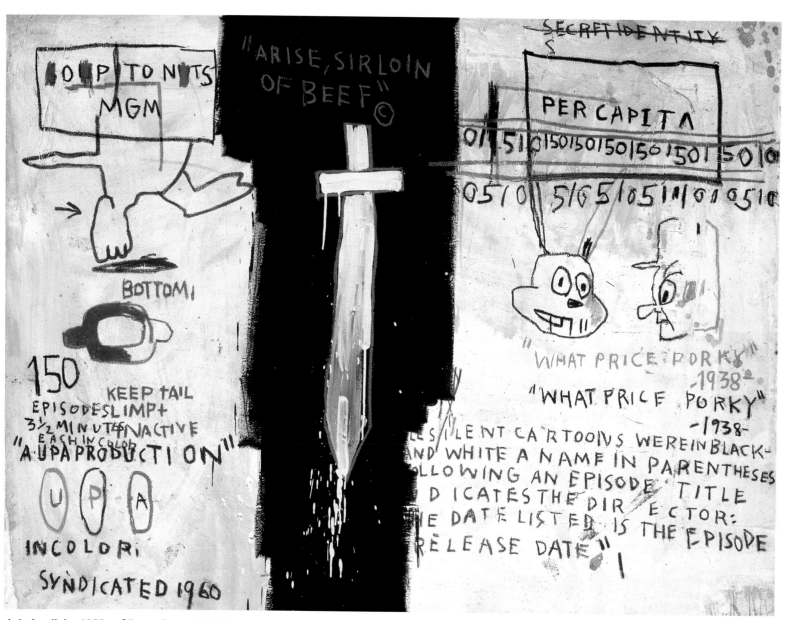

Job Analisis, 1983   Oil, acrylic and oilstick on canvas   141.6 x 187.3 cm

Untitled, 1986 Oilstick on Tyvek paper 61 x 91.5 cm

Untitled, 1986   Oilstick, pencil and color xerox on paper   75 x 105.5 cm

Untitled (Achtung), 1987   Crayon and colored pencil on paper   105.5 x 75 cm

Untitled, 1986 Pencil and colored pencil on paper 105.5 x 73.5 cm

Back of the Neck, 1983   Five color silk screen with hand painting   128 x 259 cm

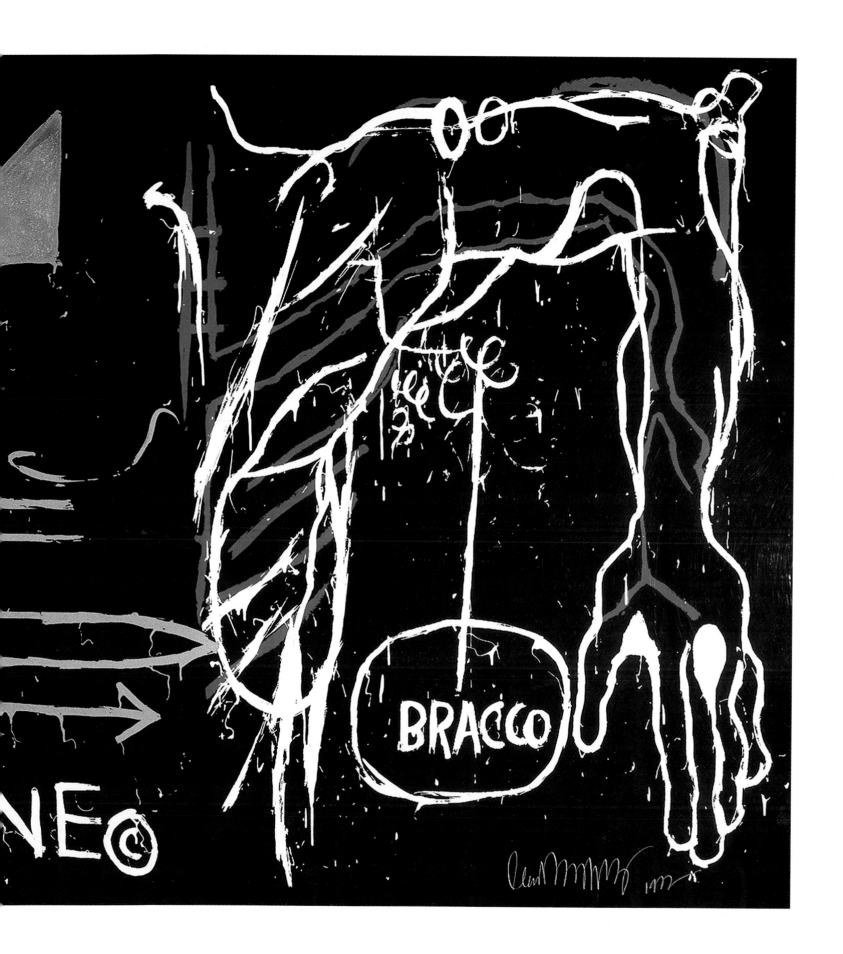

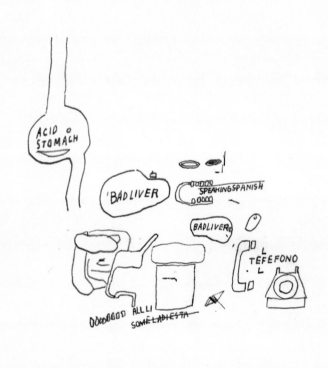

Untitled (Bad Liver, Acid Stomach), undated   Mixed media on paper   60.5 x 80.5 cm

Untitled (Themesong), 1987 Oilstick and colored pencil on paper 106.5 x 76 cm

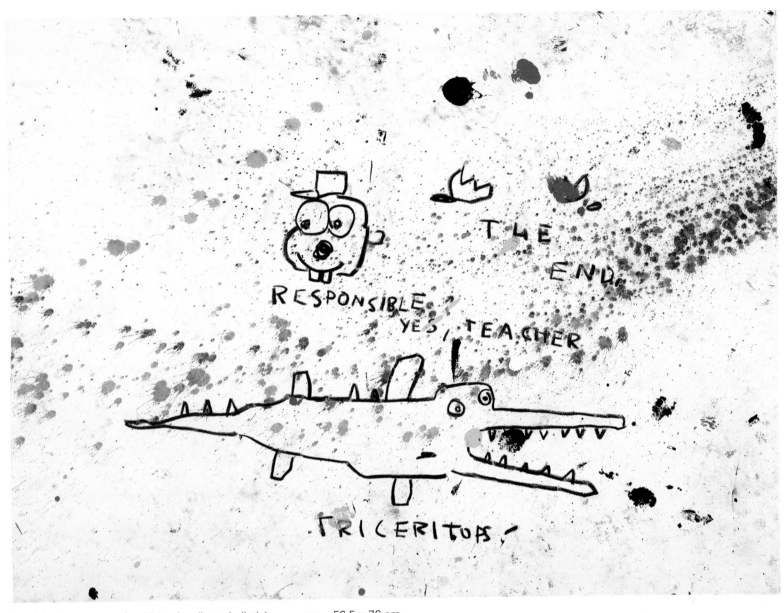

Untitled (Triceritops), 1984   Acrylic and oilstick on paper   56.5 x 76 cm

Untitled (Feet), 1984   Colored pencil on paper   61 x 46 cm

"HYDROLAGUS PURPURESCENS"

Untitled, 1984   Graphite and colored pencil on paper   21 x 27.5 cm

Untitled (Samo), 1981 Pencil on paper 22 x 15 cm

Untitled (Famous Boomerang), 1986   Oilstick, graphite, and colored pencil on paper   75 x 106 cm

Untitled, 1985   Crayon, gouache and collage on paper   56 x 76 cm

Untitled, 1984   Acrylic, watercolor and marker on paper   57 x 76 cm

A HOUSE BUILT BY FRANK LLOYD WRIGHT
FOR HIS SON ⊚ —

Untitled (Frank Lloyd Wright), 1982-83   Crayon on paper   61 x 46 cm

Untitled (Fudd), 1983 Oilstick on paper 77 x 58 cm

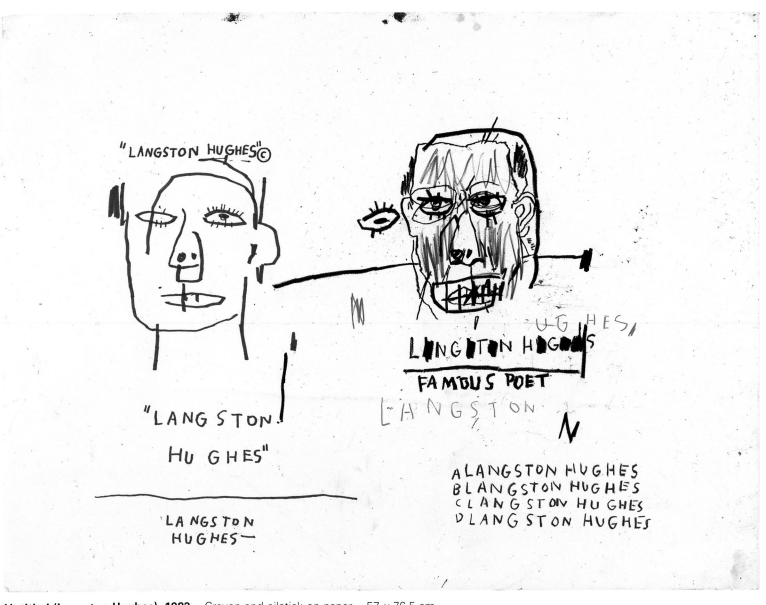

Untitled (Langston Hughes), 1983   Crayon and oilstick on paper   57 x 76.5 cm

Untitled, 1982   Oilstick and marker on paper   56.5 x 76.5 cm

Untitled (Cars/TeePees), 1981   Oilstick on paper   58.5 x 63.5 cm

Tesla vs. Edison, 1983   Charcoal and oilstick on paper   31.5 x 43.5 cm

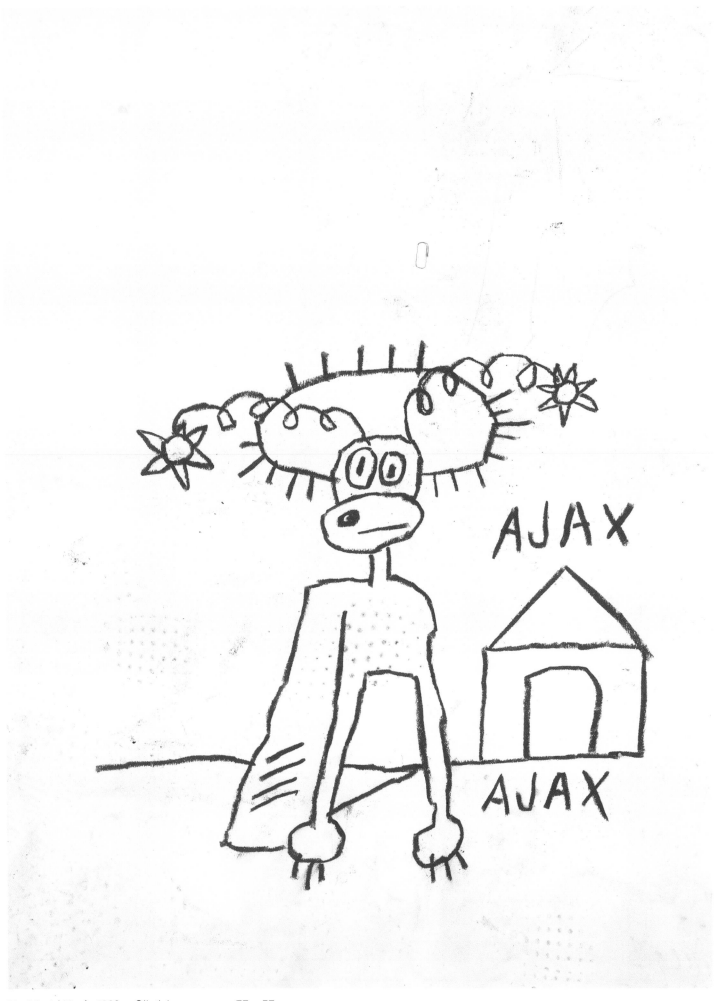

Untitled (Ajax), 1983   Oilstick on paper   77 x 57 cm

Untitled (Spin Dry), 1988   Oilstick, crayon and pencil on paper   76 x 56.5 cm

Year of the Boar, 1983   Acrylic on three connected canvases   189.9 x 243.8 cm

Jean Michel Basquiat made low culture become high art.
Pierre Restany

Jean Michel Basquiat erhob niedrige Kultur zur hohen Kunst.
Pierre Restany

Untitled (General Electric II), 1984-85
(Collaboration by Jean Michel Basquiat and Andy Warhol)
Acrylic, colored oilsticks and synthetic polymer paint silkscreened on canvas   218 x 173 cm

Untitled (A), undated   Plastic letter „A", painted with acrylic   35.5 x 17 x 3 cm

Untitled (Ass), undated   Painted spoon with oilstick   15 cm

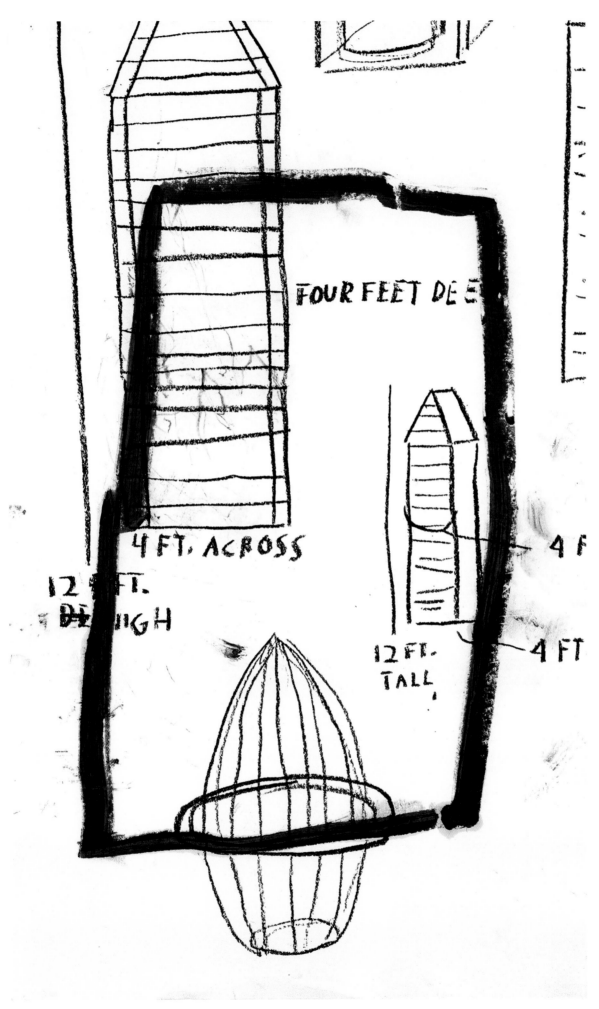

Untitled (Four Feet Across), undated Mixed media on paper 35.5 x 21 cm

Untitled (Car Freshner), undated   Mixed media on paper   70 x 100 cm

TOP Tee   JEAN MICHEL

Untitled, undated   Colored oilstick on paper   76 x 57 cm

Untitled, 1981 Oilstick on paper 76 x 56 cm

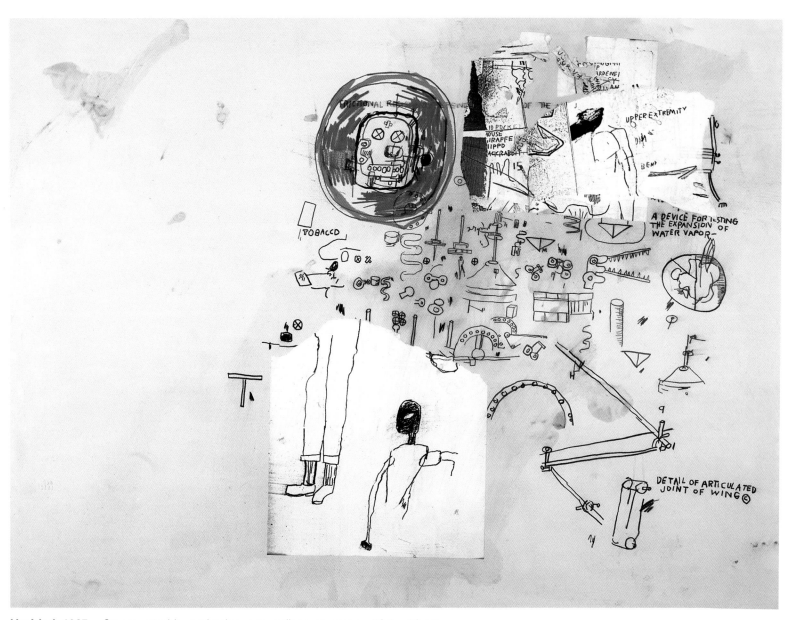

Untitled, 1985   Crayon, graphite and color xerox collage on paper   56.5 x 76 cm

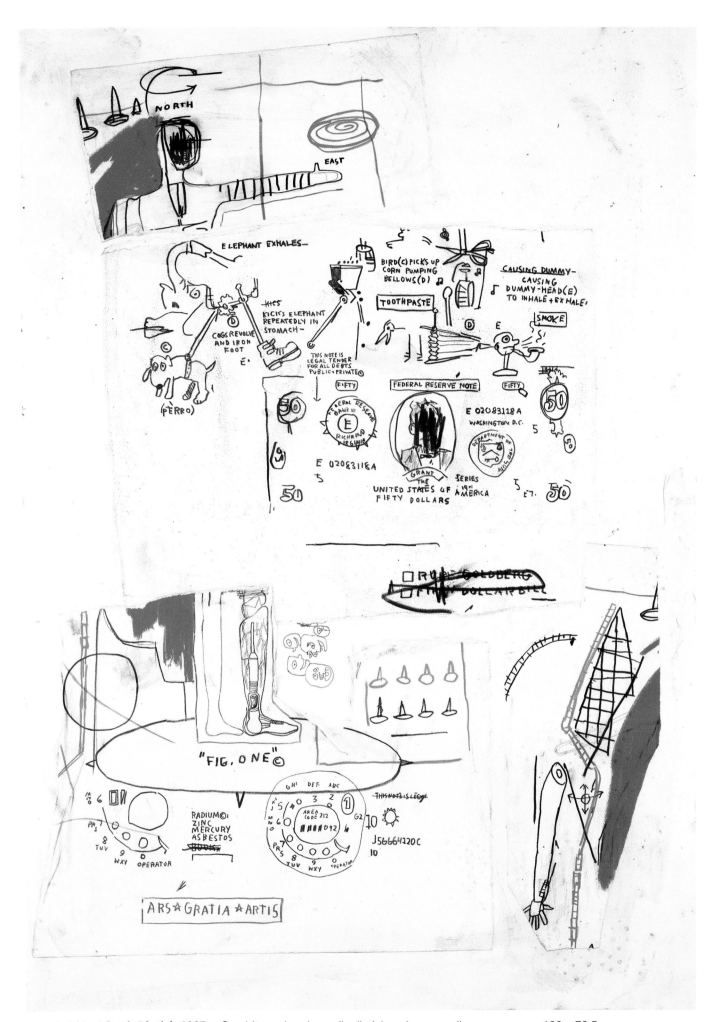

Untitled (Ars*Gratia*Artis), 1985   Graphite, colored pencil, oilstick and paper collage on paper   100 x 70.5 cm

Untitled, 1983 Watercolour, acrylic, colored crayons and paper collage on paper 100 x 70 cm

Untitled, 1983   Colored crayons, acrylic and gouache on paper   100 x 70 cm

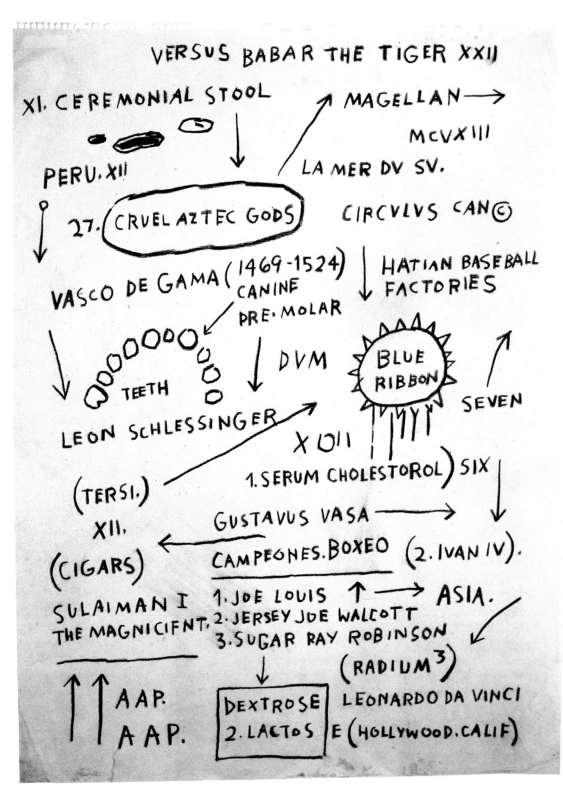

Untitled (Cruel Aztec Gods), 1983 Crayon on paper 61 x 46 cm

Untitled (Sea Monster), 1983
Oilstick on paper   61 x 46 cm

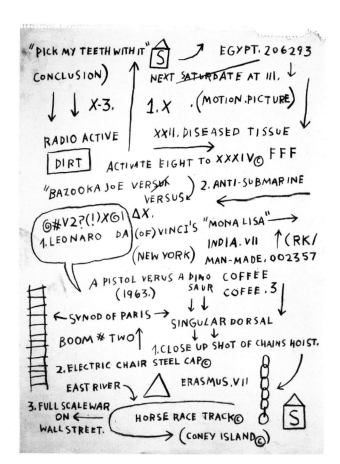

Untitled (Coney Island), 1983
Crayon on paper   61 x 46 cm

Verzeichnis ausgestellter Werke

Untitled (Car crash), 1980
Acryl, Farbspray, Marker und Firnis auf Leinwand
101,5 x 75,5 cm

Masque, 1982
Öl auf Leinwand
142 x 125 cm

Warrior, 1982
Acryl und Ölstift auf Holz
180 x 120 cm

Untitled (Football Helmet), circa 1984 (1981)
Mischtechnik (Acryl und Haar auf Football Helm)
23 x 20,5 x 33 cm

Red Kings, 1981
Acryl und Ölstift auf Holz und Glas
81 x 93,5 cm

Speaks for Itself, 1982
Triptychon, Acryl und Ölstift auf Preßfaserplatte
jeweils 122 x 122 cm

Untitled (Tar and Feathers), 1982
Acryl, Öl, Teer und Federn auf Holz
274 x 236 cm

Jersey Joe Walcott, 1982
Acryl und Ölstift auf Leinwand mit sichtbaren
Holzträgern
183 x 183 cm

Hannibal, 1982
Acryl, Ölstift und Papiercollage auf Leinwand,
montiert auf zusammengebundenen Holzträgern
152,5 x 152,5 cm

Defensive Orange, Offensive Orange, 1982
Diptychon: Acryl, Ölstift und Papier Collage auf Holz
183 x 244 cm

Untitled, 1981
Acryl und Ölkreide auf Holz
58,5 x 62 cm

Venus, 1982
Ölstift auf Leinwand
12,5 x 10 cm

Fake, 1983
Öl und Acryl auf Leinwand
214 x 214 cm

New, 1983
Öl und Acryl auf Leinwand
214 x 214 cm

Side View of an Oxen's Jaw, 1982
Acryl auf Leinwand
160 x 150 cm

Untitled (Spermatozoon), 1983
Acryl und Ölstift auf Leinwand
167,5 x 152,5 cm

Untitled (Call Girl), 1983
Acryl und Ölstift auf Leinwand
127,5 x 103 cm

Untitled, 1984
Collage und Acryl auf Leinwand
109 x 109 cm

Arteries of the Left Arm, 1983
Öl, Ölkreide und Collage auf Leinwand
160 x 150 cm

A next, 1984
Acryl, Ölstift, Klebstoff, Collage von Farbkopien
und Holz auf Holz
101,5 x 138 x 11 cm

Blue Heads, 1983
Acryl und Ölstift auf eingehängter Leinwand
183 x 234 cm

Untitled, 1981
Öl, Ölstift und Farbspray auf Leinwand
130,2 x 142,9 cm

Old Cars, 1981
Acryl, Ölstift und Papiercollage auf Leinwand
122 x 120,3 cm

Zuchero (undatiert)
Mischtechnik auf Leinwand
30,5 x 23 cm

Su Azucar (undatiert)
Mischtechnik auf Leinwand
30,5 x 23 cm

Untitled (Bicyclist), circa 1984
Mischtechnik (Öl auf Leinwand)
203 x 269 cm

Untitled (Picasso Poster), undatiert
Acryl auf Ausstellungsposter
71 x 49 cm

Boone (undatiert)
Papiercollage, Filzstift und Ölstift auf
Preßfaserplatte, aufgezogen auf Holz
104 x 30,5 cm

Maood, 1985
Acryl und Öl auf Holz
126 x 91,5 cm

Mr. Kipper, 1983
Acryl und Ölstift auf Leinwand
183 x 142 cm

Untitled (Halfmoon), 1985
Acryl und Öl auf Holz
229 x 112 cm

Untitled, 1985
Öl, Acryl, Collage von Farbkopien und
Nägel auf Holz
135 x 64 cm

Blue Skies, 1985
Acryl und Mischtechnik auf Holz
70 x 210 cm

Cash Crop, 1984
Öl und Acryl auf Leinwand
183 x 244 cm

Flexicon, 1986
Acryl, Öl und Collage auf Holz
198 x 91,5 cm

Untitled (Dodge Coupé), 1986
Acryl auf Leinwand
150 x 150 cm

Untitled, 1987
Acryl und Ölstift auf Leinwand
188 x 238,5 cm

Untitled (Ober), 1986
Acryl auf Leinwand
150 x 119,5 cm

Embittered, 1986
Collage, Bleistift und Farbe auf Holz
126 x 184 cm

Untitled (Fist), 1986
Öl und Kaffee auf Leinwand
80 x 60 cm

Untitled (Billie's Bounce), 1983
Ölstift auf Papier
80 x 59,5 cm

Untitled (Skull), 1982
Ölstift auf Papier
21,5 x 16,5 cm

Untitled, 1982
Acryl und Ölstift auf Leinen
193 x 241,5 cm

Procession, 1986
Acryl und Holzrelief auf Holz
162 x 244 cm

Untitled (Lung), 1986
Acryl auf Holz
244 x 140 cm

Life Like Son of Barney Hill
Sechs zusammen eingehängte Paneele, Acryl, Ölstift
und Collage von Farbkopien auf Leinen mit Metall-
scharnieren
122 x 522 cm

Untitled (Portrait), 1984
Ölstift und Farbstift auf Papier
76 x 56,5 cm

Untitled (Andy Warhol), 1984
Ölstift auf Papier
56,5 x 76 cm

Untitled, 1988
Acryl und Ölstift auf Leinwand
254 x 288,5 cm

Job Analisis
Öl, Acryl und Ölstift auf Leinwand
141,6 x 187,3 cm

Untitled, 1986
Ölstift auf Tyvek Papier
61 x 91,5 cm

Untitled, 1986
Ölstift, Bleistift und Farbkopien auf Papier
75 x 105,5 cm

Untitled (Achtung), 1987
Ölkreide und Farbstift auf Papier
105,5 x 75 cm

Untitled, 1986
Bleistift und Farbstift auf Papier
105,5 x 73,5 cm

Back of the Neck, 1983
Siebdruck in fünf Farben, handbemalt
128 x 259 cm

Untitled (Bad Liver/Acid Stomach), undatiert
Mischtechnik auf Papier
60,5 x 80,5 cm

Untitled (Themesong), 1987
Ölstift, Reißblei und Farbstift auf Papier
106,5 x 76 cm

Untitled (Triceritops), 1984
Acryl und Ölstift auf Papier
56,5 x 76 cm

Untitled (Feet), 1984
Farbstift auf Papier
61 x 46 cm

Untitled, 1984
Reißblei und Farbstift auf Papier
21 x 27,5 cm

Untitled (Samo), 1981
Bleistift auf Papier
22 x 15 cm

Untitled (Famous Boomerang), 1986
Ölstift, Reißblei und Farbstift auf Papier
75 x 106 cm

Untitled, 1985
Ölkreide, Gouache und Collage auf Papier
56 x 76 cm

Untitled, 1984
Acryl, Aquarell und Marker auf Papier
57 x 76 cm

Untitled (Frank Lloyd Wright), 1982-83
Ölkreide auf Papier
61 x 46 cm

Untitled (Fudd), 1983
Ölstift auf Papier
77 x 58 cm

Untitled (Langston Hughes), 1983
Ölkreide und Ölstift auf Papier
57 x 76,5 cm

Untitled, 1982
Ölstift und Marker auf Papier
56,5 x 76,5 cm

Untitled (Cars/Teepees), 1981
Ölstift auf Papier
58,5 x 63,5 cm

Tesla vs. Edison, 1983
Kohle und Ölstift auf Papier
31,5 x 43,5 cm

Untitled (Ajax), 1983
Ölstift auf Papier
77 x 57 cm

Untitled (Spin Dry), 1988
Ölstift, Ölkreide und Bleistift auf Papier
76 x 56,5 cm

Year of the Boar
Acryl auf drei verbundenen Leinwandstreifen
189,9 x 243,8 cm

Untitled (General Electric II), 1984-85
(Jean-Michel Basquiat und Andy Warhol)
Acryl, farbige Ölstifte und Kunststofffarbe im Siebdruck auf Leinwand
218 x 173 cm

Untitled (A), undatiert
Plastikbuchstabe »A«, bemalt mit Acryl
35,5 x 17 x 3 cm

Untitled (Ass), undatiert
Ölstift auf einem Löffel
15 cm

Untitled (Four Feet Across), undatiert
Mischtechnik auf Papier
35,5 x 21 cm

Untitled (Car Freshner), undatiert
Mischtechnik auf Papier
70 x 100 cm

Untitled (undatiert)
Ölstift auf Papier
76 x 57 cm

Untitled, 1981
Ölstift auf Papier
76 x 56 cm

Untitled, 1985
Ölkreide, Reißblei und Collage von Farbkopien
auf Papier
56,5 x 76 cm

Untitled (Ars*Gratia*Artis), 1985
Reißblei, Farbstift, Ölstift und Papiercollage
auf Papier
100 x 70,5 cm

Untitled, 1983
Aquarell, Acryl, Ölkreide und
Papiercollage auf Papier
100 x 70 cm

Untitled, 1983
Ölkreide, Acryl und Gouache auf Papier
100 x 70 cm

Untitled (Cruel Aztec Gods), 1983
Ölkreide auf Papier
61 x 46 cm

Untitled (Sea Monster), 1983
Ölstift auf Papier
61 x 46 cm

Untitled (Coney Island), 1983
Ölkreide auf Papier
61 x 46 cm

Anhang

Appendix

Biographie

Zusammengestellt von Jacob Baal-Teshuva

1960 Geburt Jean Michel Basquiats in Brooklyn am 22. Dezember. Seine Mutter Matilde, deren Eltern aus Puerto Rico eingewandert sind, ist in Brooklyn geboren. Der Vater, Gerard, stammt aus Port-au-Prince, Haiti.

1963 Geburt der Schwester Lisane, ebenfalls in Brooklyn.

1964 Der Vater, der als Buchhalter arbeitet, bringt Papier nach Hause, damit der Sohn und seine Frau darauf zeichnen können. Die Mutter, die sich für Modedesign interessiert, zeichnet zusammen mit dem Sohn, der seine Anregungen aus dem Fernsehen und aus Hitchcock-Filmen schöpft.

1965 Jean Michel wird oft von der Mutter ins Brooklyn Museum, Metropolitan Museum und Museum of Modern Art in Manhattan geführt. Die Mutter hat einen ermunternden Einfluß auf seine Kunst und Bildung, wie Basquiat Jahre später einräumt.

1966 Geburt einer weiteren Schwester, Jeanine, in Brooklyn.

1967 Basquiat besucht eine katholische Privatschule, Saint Ann's. Zusammen mit einem Schulfreund schreibt und illustriert er ein Kinderbuch. Wegen der Herkunft seiner Familie spricht und liest er Spanisch, Französisch und Englisch. Er interessiert sich auch für Sport.

1968 Beim Ballspiel mit Freunden auf der Straße wird er von einem vorbeifahrenden Auto erfaßt. Basquiat bricht sich den Arm, erleidet verschiedene innere Verletzungen und verbringt einen Monat im Krankenhaus. Das Buch »Grays Anatomie«, das ihm die Mutter während der Genesung schenkt, macht einen tiefen Eindruck auf ihn und beeinflußt seine frühen Zeichnungen. In diesem Jahr – Basquiat ist erst sieben – trennen sich die Eltern. Zusammen mit den beiden Schwestern lebt er beim Vater.

1974–75 Basquiats Vater zieht mit den drei Kindern nach Puerto Rico, wo er einen neuen Job bekommen hat. Kurze Zeit später läuft der sich stets gegen die väterliche Disziplin auflehnende Jean Michel von zu Hause weg, wird aber von Fremden nach Hause gebracht.

1976 Noch einmal nimmt der Vater eine neue Stelle an und kehrt mit den Kindern nach Brooklyn zurück, wo Jean Michel die »High School« beginnt, um später in eine Schule für begabte Kinder überzuwechseln. Dort lernt er den Graffiti-Künstler Al Diaz kennen. Sie werden Freunde und arbeiten auch zusammen. Im

Basquiat in der Akira Ikeda Gallery am 9. November 1985 (Foto: Yoshitaka Uchida, Tokyo)

Basquiat in der Akira Ikeda Gallery am
9. November 1985 (Foto: Yoshitaka Uchida, Tokyo)

Chronology

Compiled by Jacob Baal-Teshuva

1960   Jean Michel Basquiat is born in Brooklyn on 22 December. His mother Matilde, first generation Puerto Rican, was born in Brooklyn. His father Gerard was born in Port-au-Prince, Haiti.

1963   His sister Lisane was born, also in Brooklyn.

1964   His father who worked as an accountant brings home paper for his son and wife to draw. His mother who was interested in fashion design kept drawing together with her son who was inspired by television images, and Hitchcock films.

1965   Jean Michel was often taken by his mother to visit the Brooklyn Museum, the Metropolitan Museum, and the Museum of Modern Art in Manhattan. His mother, was a source of encouragement to her son in art and education, which Basquiat acknowledged years later.

1966   Jeanine, a second sister is born in Brooklyn.

1967   Basquiat attends a private Catholic School, Saint Ann's. Together with a friend in school, he wrote and illustrated a children's book. Because of his family's background, he spoke and read Spanish, French, and English. He was also interested in sports.

1968   While playing ball with friends on the street, he is hit by a car. Basquiat breaks an arm, suffers various internal injuries, and is hospitalized for a month. The book *Gray's Anatomy* which he receives from his mother during his convalescence, impresses him and influences his early drawings. That year, while he is seven years old, his parents separate. Together with his two sisters, he lives with his father.

1974–75 Basquiat's father moves with his three children for a new job to Puerto-Rico. Shortly later Jean Michel, who did not like discipline, runs away from home, but he is returned by strangers.

1976   Again his father changes jobs and returns with his children to Brooklyn where Jean Michel enters high school, and later a special school for gifted children. It was there that he met Al Diaz, a graffiti artist. They became friends and collaborators. In December Basquiat, age 15, runs away from home again, for two weeks. His father finally finds him in Washington Square Park, in Greenwich Village. His first ambition, according to one of this text drawings, was to become a fireman, while his first artistic ambition was to be a cartoonist. Among his early themes are: the seaview from the film »Voyage to the Bottom of the Sea«, Alfred E. Newman, from *Mad Magazine*, the film director Alfred Hitchcock, whom he was drawing several times. Other subjects were: President Nixon,

Dezember läuft Basquiat, nunmehr 15jährig, noch einmal von zu Hause weg, diesmal für zwei Wochen. Sein Vater findet ihn endlich im Washington Square Park, in der Nähe von Greenwich Village. Sein erstes Lebensziel ist, wie aus einer seiner erzählenden Zeichnungen hervorgeht, Feuerwehrmann zu werden, während er künstlerisch zunächst Karikaturist werden will. Zu seinen frühen Themen gehören: die Meeresaussicht aus dem Film »Reise zum Grund des Meeres«, Alfred E. Newman aus dem »Mad Magazine«, der Filmregisseur Alfred Hitchcock, den er öfter zeichnete. Andere Themen: Präsident Nixon, Autos, der Krieg, Waffen. Als Drittkläßler schickt er J. Edgar Hoover, damals noch Chef der FBI, die Zeichnung einer Schußwaffe, erhält aber keine Antwort. Nach Aussage Basquiats zählen zu seinen frühen musikalischen Einflüssen das Musical »West Side Story«, »Round 'bout Midnight«, »Walking Harry« und der Film »Orphée negro«.

Jean Michel Basquiat, Samo, 1978
Tinte auf Papier, 30,5 x 22,9 cm

1977 Während seiner Zeit in der City School for Gifted Children entwickelt Basquiat ein Interesse für das Theater und erfindet eine fiktive Figur, der er den Namen Samo (von »same old shit«) gibt, die davon lebt, Ersatzreligion unter die Leute zu bringen. Basquiat und sein Freund Diaz beginnen, Züge und Mauern im unteren Manhattan mit Farbe zu besprühen. Sie kreieren Bilder und Inschriften voll Witz und Humor.

1978 Ein Jahr vor dem Schulabschluß verläßt Basquiat die Schule. Er zieht von zu Hause weg und findet Unterschlupf bei verschiedenen Freunden. Um Geld zu verdienen, verkauft er handbemalte T-Shirts und Postkarten. Erste Begegnungen mit Andy Warhol und Henry Geldzahler, den er in einem Restaurant in Soho anspricht. Er wird zu einer vertrauten Erscheinung unter den Musikern, Filmemachern, Sängern und Künstlern, die er in verschiedenen Clubs kennenlernt: im Mudd Club, Club 57, Hurrah und Tier 3. Die Ausgabe der Wochenzeitung »Village Voice« vom 11. Dezember macht erstmals auf die mit Samo gezeichneten Graffiti aufmerksam.

1979 Zerwürfnis zwischen Basquiat und seinem Freund Al Diaz: ihre Zusammenarbeit als »Samo« und die Freundschaft sind zu Ende. Plötzlich sind die Mauern von Soho und der East Village voll mit Aufschriften: »Samo ist tot«. Basquiat bemalt weiterhin T-Shirts und Postkarten, die er auf der Straße im Washington Square Park und vor den Museen verkauft. Im Mai tut er sich mit den Freunden Michael Holman, Sharon Dawson und Vincent Gallo zu einer Band zusammen, die den Namen »Channel 9« bekommt. Später wird die Band zweimal umbenannt, erst zu »Test Pattern« und dann, als Nicholas Taylor und Justin Thyme hinzukommen, zu »Gray«. Basquiat, der ein begabter Musiker ist, spielt Klarinette und Synthesizer. Im Herbst lernt er die Künstler-Kollegen Keith Haring und

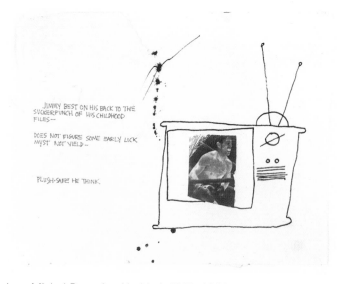

Jean Michel Basquiat, Untitled, 1980–1981
Tinte und Kollage auf Papier, 17,2 x 22,9 cm

Basquiat in der Galerie Bruno Bischofberger, Zürich 1982
(Foto: Beth Phillips)

Warhol, Basquiat, Bischofberger und Clemente in New York,
1984 (Foto: Beth Phillips)

Basquiat mit Bruno Bischofberger in dessen Galerie in Zürich,
1985 (Foto: Beth Phillips)

cars, wars and weapons. While in the third grade in school, he sent a drawing of a gun to J. Edgar Hoover, director of the FBI, but never got a reply. According to Basquiat his early music influences were: the musical »West Side Story«, »Round 'bout Midnight«, »Walking Harry«, and the film »Black Orpheus«.

1977   While attending the high school City-as-School for gifted children, Basquiat gets interested in the theatre, and creates a fictional character which he calls »Samo« (same old shit) who makes a living selling fake religion. Basquiat and his friend Diaz start doing spray-paintings on trains and walls around lower Manhattan. These consist of drawings and writings full of wit and humor.

1978   Basquiat drops out of high school a year before graduation. He leaves home and stays at the homes of various friends. In order to earn money, he starts to sell hand made T-shirts and painted postcards. He first meets Andy Warhol and Henry Geldzahler, whom he approaches in a Soho restaurant. He becomes a regular face among musicians, film makers, singers and artists whom he met in various clubs, such as: Mudd Club, Club 57, Hurrah, and Tier 3. First attention to the wall graffiti signed »Samo«, appeared on 11 December at the Village Voice weekly Journal.

1979   Basquiat and his friend Al Diaz had a falling out which ends their »Samo« collaboration and friendship. Suddenly the walls of Soho and East Village were covered with the signs of »Samo is dead«. Basquiat continues to paint postcards and T-shirts, which he sells on the street in Washington Square Park and in front of Museums. In May he joins his friend Michael Holman, Sharon Dawson, and Vincent Gallo to form a music band which they name »Channel 9«. Later, twice, they change the band's name, first to »Test Pattern«, and then to »Gray«, when Nicholas Taylor and Justin Thyme joined the band. Basquiat, who was a talented musician, played the clarinet and a synthesizer. In the fall he meets fellow artists Keith Haring and Kenny Scharf, who were part of the art and graffiti scene in the East Village, Soho and its clubs such as Club 57. Another person he met was Glenn O'Brien, who was music editor for *Interview Magazine*, and a producer of a program on Cable TV. They became good friends and he often invites Basquiat to appear on his TV show. It was through Diego Cortez, a film maker whom he met at the Mudd Club, that he was introduced to Henry Geldzahler, who was then Chief curator of Twentieth Century Art at the Metropolitan Museum of Art.

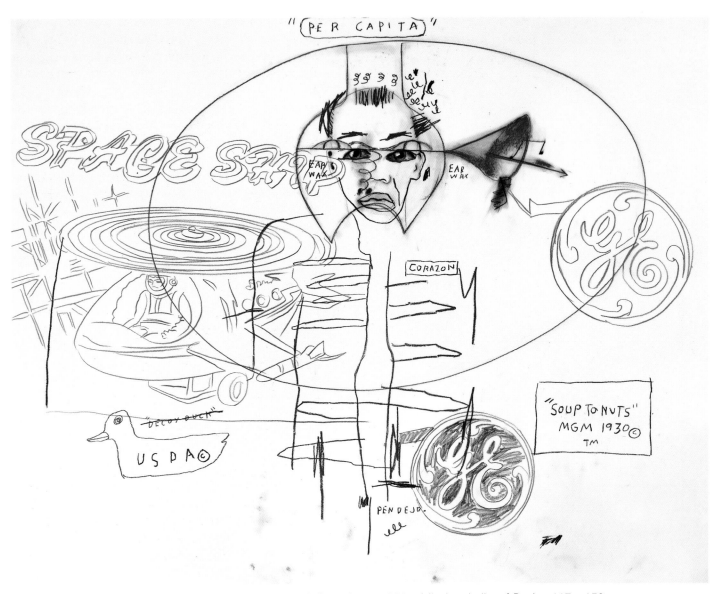

Jean Michel Basquiat, Francesco Clemente, Andy Warhol: Saxophone, 1984   Mischtechnik auf Papier, 117 x 150 cm

Kenny Scharf kennen, die zur Kunst- und Graffiti-Szene in der East Village, Soho und den dort befindlichen Clubs gehören, wie beispielsweise Club 57. Außerdem lernt er Glenn O'Brien kennen, der die Musikredaktion des »Interview Magazine« leitet und eine Sendung im Kabelfernsehen produziert. Sie werden gute Freunde, und er lädt Basquiat oft ein, in seiner TV-Sendung aufzutreten. Durch Diego Cortez, einen Filmemacher, den er im Mudd Club kennengelernt hat, wird er Henry Geldzahler vorgestellt, der zu dieser Zeit Kurator für Kunst des 20. Jahrhunderts im Metropolitan Museum of Art ist.

1980   Im Juni wird die Kunst Basquiats erstmals ausgestellt – in der »Times Square Show«-Gruppenausstellung, die in einem leerstehenden Gebäude am Times Square veranstaltet wird. Zu den weiteren Künstlern zählen: Jenny Holzer, Kenny Scharf, Kiki Smith. Als Folge des Erfolges dieser Ausstellung und der neuen Anerkennung als Künstler verläßt Basquiat die Band »Gray«, die sich kurze Zeit später auflöst.

1980 In the month of June the art of Basquiat is exhibited for the first time in a group exhibition, »The Times Square Show«. It was held in an empty building in Times Square. Among the other artists participating are: Jenny Holzer, Kenny Scharf, and Kiki Smith. As a result of the success of the show, and his recognition as an artist, Basquiat leaves the Gray Band which disbanded a short time later. His friend Glenn O'Brien asks Basquiat to play the leading role in a film »New York Beat« written by O'Brien, produced by Maripol, and directed by Edo Bertoglio. The film, which was never released, was to depict in some way the art scene with Basquiat as the star. It was O'Brien who introduced Basquiat to Andy Warhol. With money he earned from the film he bought art supplies enabling him to paint. He sells his first canvases for $ 100.

1981 In February, Basquiat is invited to exhibit in »New York/New Wave«, an exhibition at P. S. 1 the Institute for Art and Urban Resources on Long Island, organized by Diego Cortez. Twenty artists participated in this show including Andy Warhol, Keith Haring, Robert Mapplethorpe, Kenny Scharf, Fab 5/Freddy (Braithwaite) and some graffiti artists. Subsequently Keith Haring organizes the »Lower Manhattan Drawing Show« at the Mudd Club. This is followed in April by Futura 2000 and Fred Braithwaite in the Mudd Club in an exhibition entitled »Beyond Words: Graffiti Based-Rooted–Inspired Works«. They include works of Basquiat from the Samo period. In May Basquiat leaves for Europe for the first time to exhibit his first one man show at the Galleria d'Arte Emilio Mazzoli in Modena, Italy. The work is shown with the name

Ausstellung: Jean Michel Basquiat, Galerie Yvon Lambert, Paris, 1988 (Foto: Konstaninos Ignatiadis)

Glenn O'Brien bittet ihn, die Hauptrolle in einem Film, »New York Beat«, zu spielen, zu dem O'Brien das Buch geschrieben hat (produziert von Maripol; Regie: Edo Bertoglio). Der Film, der nie freigegeben wurde, sollte irgendwie die Kunstszene darstellen, mit Basquiat als Hauptakteur. Es ist O'Brien, der Basquiat Andy Warhol vorstellt. Mit dem Geld, das er bei den Dreharbeiten verdient hat, kauft er sich Malermaterialien und kann nun malen. Er verkauft seine ersten Bilder für $ 100.

1981   Im Februar wird Basquiat eingeladen, sich an der Ausstellung »New York/New Wave« zu beteiligen, die im P. S. 1, Institut für Kunst und städtische Ressourcen, unter der Leitung von Diego Cortez auf Long Island veranstaltet wird. Zwanzig Künstler sind daran beteiligt, darunter Andy Warhol, Keith Haring, Robert Mapplethorpe, Kenny Scharf, Fab 5 Freddy (Braithwaite) und einige Graffiti-Künstler. Etwas später führt Keith Haring die »Lower Manhattan Drawing Show« im Mudd Club durch, gefolgt im April von »Futura 2000«, und einer von Fred Braithwaite im Mudd-Club organisierten Ausstellung »Beyond Words: Graffiti Based-Rooted-Inspired Works«, darunter Werke Basquiats aus der Samo-Periode. Im Mai reist Basquiat zum erstenmal nach Europa, um seine erste Einzelausstellung abzuhalten: in der Galleria d'Arte Emilio Mazzoli in Modena/Italien. Die Arbeiten werden mit dem Namen Samo ausgestellt. Nach der Rückkehr in die USA lädt ihn die Kunsthändlerin Annina Nosei ein, an der Ausstellung »Public Address« in ihrer Galerie teilzunehmen. Als Folge dieser Zusammenarbeit wird Annina Nosei die Hauptgaleristin Basquiats. Da sie weiß, daß er kein eigenes Atelier hat, bietet sie ihm dazu die Benutzung ihres Kellers an. Der erste Aufsatz über Basquiat erscheint in der Zeitschrift »Artforum« unter dem Titel »The Radiant Child« (Kind mit Ausstrahlung), von René Richard. Darin werden »die Eleganz Twomblys« sowie die »Art brut des jungen Dubuffet« als Einflüsse angeführt.

1982   Im März findet die erste Einzelausstellung in den USA in der Annina Nosei Gallery statt. Sie wird ein Riesenerfolg. Die Zeitschriften »Art in America« und »Flash Art« berichten positiv darüber. Nach einer Beteiligung an einer Gruppenausstellung in Modena, »Transavanguardia Italia/America« mit Sandro Chia, Francesco Clemente, Enzo Cucchi, David Salle, Julian Schnabel u. a. reist Basquiat nach Los Angeles für eine Einzelausstellung in der Larry Gagosian Gallery. Er bleibt sechs Monate in Los Angeles. Im Juni wird Basquiat, ganze 21 Jahre alt, der jüngste von 176 Künstlern, die zur Teilnahme an der international renommierten »Documenta 7« in Kassel aufgefordert werden. Auf Drängen von Annina Nosei schafft er seine erste Druckgrafik, eine Mappe mit dem Titel »Anatomie«. Sie umfaßt 18 Siebdrucke, die Nosei veröffentlicht. Im September stellt er erstmals in der

Jean Michel Basquiat, Andy Warhol: Socialite, 1984
Acryl auf Leinwand, 193 x 263 cm

Jean Michel Basquiat, Andy Warhol: Motorbike, 1985
Acryl auf Leinwand, 195 x 452 cm

Jean Michel Basquiat, Andy Warhol: Win $ 1,000,000, 1984
Acryl auf Leinwand, 173 x 290 cm

Samo. Upon his return to the US the art dealer Anni-na Nosei invites Basquiat to take part in a group show in her gallery in September entitled »Public Address«. As a result of this show, Annina Nosei becomes Bas-quiats' main dealer. Knowing that he did not have a studio of his own, she invites him to use her base-ment space to work. The first article on Basquiat ent-itled »The Radiant Child« by René Richard is published in *Artforum*. He mentions the influences of »The Ele-gance of Twombly« and »The Brut of the Young Dubuffet«.

1982   In March he has his first one man show exhibition in the U.S. at Annina Nosei Gallery. It is a big success. *Art in America* and *Flash Art magazines* comment favorably on the show. After exhibiting in a group show in Modena, Italy, »Transavanguardia Italia/Ame-rica,« including the artists Sandro Chia, Francesco Cle-mente, Enzo Cucchi, David Salle, and Julian Schnabel, Basquiat goes to Los Angeles for his one man show at the Larry Gagosian Gallery. He remains in Los Ange-les for six months. In June, Basquiat becomes the youngest of 176 artists at age 21 to be invited to exhi-bit in the internationally prestigious »Documenta 7« in Kassel, Germany. At the urging of Annina Nosei, he creates his first prints in a portfolio entitled »Ana-tomy«. It contains 18 silk-screens published by Ms. Nosei. In September he exhibits for the first time at Galerie Bruno Bischofberger in Zurich, Switzerland. In November he has a one man show at »Fun Gallery« in the East Village. He exhibited there despite the objec-tion of his dealer Annina Nosei. This brought about the end of Basquiat's relationship with his first dealer. In December he has a first one man show at the Galerie Delta in Rotterdam, Holland. Basquiat, whose interest in music continues, produces a record of Rap Music entitled »Beat Bop« with Fred Braithwaite, Toxic, A-one, Al Diaz, Rammellzee, and a few others. He spends part of winter 1982-83 in Los Angeles where he returns annually. He often meets there with Mr. Chow, owner of the most famous Chinese restaurant and a well known art collector. Basquiat gives Mr. Michael Chow paintings in exchange for his food and drinks at the restaurant. He produces in California five editions of prints with the help of Los Angeles dealer Fred Hoffman.

1983   Basquiat goes back to Los Angeles for his second exhibition at Larry Gagosian Gallery. He is also includ-ed in the 1983 Biennial Exhibition at the Whitney Museum of American Art in New York. In August Basquiat rents a building on Great Jones Street from Andy Warhol. Their relationship becomes close. Basquiat sees Warhol as a role model, mentor, and a great influence. On September 5 1983 Andy Warhol notes in his diaries, edited by Pat Hackett, »Jean Michel called, he wanted some philosophy, he came over and we talked, and he's afraid he's just going to

Galerie Bruno Bischofberger in Zürich aus. Im November folgt eine Einzelausstellung in der »Fun Gallery« im East Village. Er stellt dort trotz der Proteste Annina Noseis aus, wodurch seine Beziehungen zu seiner ersten Galeristin beendet sind. Im Dezember hat er seine erste Einzelausstellung in der Galerie Delta in Rotterdam. Basquiat, der sich weiterhin für die Musik interessiert, produziert eine Schallplatte mit Rapmusik, »Beat Bop«, mit Fred Braithwaite, Toxic, A-one, Al Diaz, Rammellzee und einigen anderen. Er verbringt einen Teil des Winters 1982–83 in Los Angeles, wohin er auch jedes Jahr zurückkehrt. Er trifft sich dort oft mit Mr. Chow, Besitzer des bekanntesten China-Restaurants der Stadt und ein bekannter Kunstsammler. Um seine Zeche an Speisen und Getränken im Restaurant von Mr. Michael Chow zu begleichen, gibt Basquiat ihm Gemälde im Tauschgeschäft. Mit Hilfe des in Los Angeles wirkenden Kunsthändlers Fred Hoffman bringt Basquiat fünf Druckgrafik-Serien heraus.

1983   Basquiat kehrt für seine zweite Ausstellung in der Larry Gagosian Gallery nach Los Angeles zurück. Er gehört auch zu den Künstlern, die für die 1983er Biennale des Whitney Museum of American Art in

Ausstellung: Jean Michel Basquiat, Whitney Museum of American Art, New York, 1992/93

be a flash in the pan, and I told him not to worry, that he wouldn't be. But then I got scared because he's rented our building on Great Jones and what if he is a flash in the pan and doesn't have the money to pay his rent?«. In November at the urging of Bruno Bischofberger, Basquiat, Warhol, and Clemente, start working on collaborative paintings in New York. He also collaborated, later, with Andy Warhol alone, and they produced 50–60 paintings. In December he returns to Los Angeles, where he spends time with Madonna, whom he knew from New York and the Mudd Club.

1984   Basquiat goes from Los Angeles to Hawaii, to the island of Maui. He rents a ranch in a remote area, and starts a new studio to which he returns often. In March he returns to New York, and despite his apprehension in joining another dealer, he starts a relationship with Mary Boone Gallery in Soho where he has his first one man show in May. A contemporary auction at Christie's in May includes a 1981 Basquiat untitled painting that sells for $ 19.000. The same painting was purchased a year earlier for $ 4,000. (In 1988 a Basquiat painting sells at Sotheby's for over half a million dollars). The first museum exhibition of

New York ausgewählt werden. Im August mietet Basquiat ein Gebäude in der Great Jones Street von Andy Warhol. Ihre Beziehungen werden enger. Basquiat betrachtet Warhol als Vorbild, Mentor und großen Einfluß. Am 5. September 1983 schreibt Andy Warhol in seinem Tagebuch, in der von Pat Hackett betreuten Ausgabe: »Jean Michel hat angerufen, er brauchte ein wenig Philosophie; er kam vorbei und wir redeten. Er hat Angst, daß er bloß ein Strohfeuer gewesen sei, und ich sagte ihm, er solle sich keine Sorgen machen, das wäre er nicht. Aber dann packte mich die Angst, denn er hat unser Gebäude in der Great Jones Street gemietet, und was geschieht dann, wenn er tatsächlich bloß ein Strohfeuer ist und die Miete nicht bezahlen kann?« Auf Drängen von Bruno Bischofberger beginnen Basquiat, Warhol und Clemente im November in New York die Arbeit an gemeinsamen Gemälden. Später wird Basquiat mit Andy Warhol allein zusammenarbeiten; auf diese Weise kommen 50 bis 60 Gemälde zustande. Im Dezember kehrt er nach Los Angeles zurück, wo er mit Madonna Umgang pflegt, die er von New York und dem Mudd Club her kennt.

1984 Basquiat geht von Los Angeles nach Hawaii, auf die Insel Maui. Er mietet eine Ranch in einem entlegenen Gebiet und gründet ein neues Atelier, zu dem er oft zurückkehrt. Im März kehrt er nach New York zurück, wo er trotz seiner Skepsis, sich mit einem Galeristen zusammenzutun, eine Beziehung zur Mary Boone Gallery in Soho eingeht, in der eine erste Einzelausstellung im Mai durchgeführt wird. Zu dieser Zeit findet eine Versteigerung bei Christie's statt, in der ein untituliertes Gemälde Basquiats aus dem Jahre 1981 für $ 19 000 erworben wird. Dasselbe Gemälde war ein Jahr zuvor für $ 4 000 gekauft worden. (1988 wird ein Gemälde Basquiats bei Sotheby für mehr als eine halbe Million Dollar den Besitzer wechseln.) Die erste Museumsausstellung Basquiats wird im August in der Fruitmarket Gallery in Edinburgh eröffnet. Die von Warhol und Basquiat gemeinsam ausgeführten Gemälde werden in der Galerie Bruno Bischofsberger in Zürich gezeigt.

1985 Im Januar findet eine Einzelausstellung in der Galerie Bruno Bischofberger in Zürich statt. Basquiat wird auf der Titelseite des »New York Times Magazine« (Ausgabe vom 10. Februar) abgebildet. Im März eine zweite Einzelausstellung in der Mary Boone Gallery. Im Mai wird Basquiat zusammen mit Francesco Clemente, Keith Haring und Kenny Scharf beauftragt, Wandgemälde im neuen Palladium Club in der East 14th Street in New York auszuführen. Im September werden sechzehn gemeinsame Bilder von Warhol und Basquiat in der Tony Shafrazi Gallery in Soho ausgestellt. Für die Plakate zur Ausstellung posieren Warhol und Basquiat auf Anregung Shafrazis mit Boxhandschuhen. Die Gemälde finden in der Presse heftige Ablehnung, und nur eines wird verkauft. Die negativen Kritiken führen zu einer Spannung zwischen Basquiat

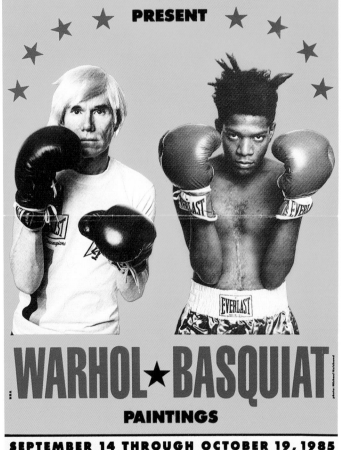

Ausstellungsposter »Warhol - Basquiat, Paintings«, Tony Shafrazi Gallery, 1985

Keith Haring, A Pile of Crowns for Jean Michel Basquiat, 1988

Bernard Rancilc, Jean Michel Basquiat, 1998

Basquiat opens in August at the Fruitmarket Gallery in Edinburgh, Scotland. The collaborative paintings of Warhol-Basquiat are shown at Galerie Bischofberger in Zurich, Switzerland.

1985   In January he has a one man show at Galerie Bruno Bischofberger in Zurich, Switzerland. Basquiat appears February 10th on the cover of the New York Times Magazine. Second one man show in March at Mary Boone's Gallery. In May Basquiat, together with the artists Francesco Clemente, Keith Haring and Kenny Scharf is commissioned to paint two murals at the new Paladium Club on East 14th Street in New York. In September, sixteen collaborative paintings by Warhol and Basquiat are exhibited at the Tony Shafrazi Gallery in Soho. For the poster of the show both artists, Warhol and Basquiat posed at Shafrazi's request with boxing gloves. The paintings were severely criticized in the press, and only one painting was sold. The negative reviews caused tension between Basquiat and Warhol, it weakened their relationship. In December Basquiat flew to Tokyo for the opening of his one man show at the Akira Ikeda Gallery.

1986   In January Basquiat goes to Los Angeles for two weeks, for what was his last exhibition at Larry Gagosian Gallery. In August he travels to Africa for the first time. There he is joined by his dealer Bruno Bischofberger who arranged, at Basquiat's request, an exhibition in Abidjan, the Ivory Coast. Basquiat's relationship with Mary Boone takes a turn for the worse, by December he leaves the gallery and again he is without a dealer. In November, an exhibition of Basquiat's work opens at the Kestner-Gesellschaft, in Hanover, Germany. It consisted of about sixty works.

1987   Basquiat has a January one man show of 12 paintings at Daniel Templon Gallery in Paris. The death of Andy Warhol on the 22nd of February shocks Basquiat, and leaves him devastated despite the deteriorated relationship between them in the last year. He paints a gravestone and portraits of Warhol, as a memorial to his friend. In May he exhibits three large works on paper at the Tony Shafrazi Gallery in Soho.

1988   For his one man show at the Yvon Lambert Gallery in Paris, Basquiat goes to Paris, and later also exhibits at Galerie Hans Mayer in Dusseldorf, Germany. Basquiat returns to New York for an exhibition in April at Vrej Baghoomian Gallery. Basquiat used drugs and always resisted treatment for drugs. But before leaving for Dallas, and Los Angeles on the way to his ranch in Maui, Hawaii, he tells his assistant that he got rid of drugs for good. On Friday the 12th of August Basquiat dies in his Great Jones Street House at the age of 27. An autopsy report listed the cause of death as »acute mixed drug intoxication«. A private funeral was held on August 17 in New York at the Frank E. Campbell Funeral Chapel. His immediate family and close friends attended. Among them were Keith Haring, Francesco

und Warhol und schwächen ihre Beziehung. Im Dezember fliegt Basquiat nach Tokio zur Eröffnung der Einzelausstellung in der Akira Ikeda Gallery.

1986 Im Januar reist Basquiat für zwei Wochen nach Los Angeles zur, wie es sich herausstellt, letzten Ausstellung in der Larry Gagosian Gallery. Im August reist er zum erstenmal nach Afrika. Dort trifft er seinen Galeristen Bruno Bischofberger, der auf Bitten Basquiats eine Ausstellung in Abidjan, Elfenbeinküste, zusammenstellt. Basquiats Beziehung zu Mary Boone verschlechtert sich; im Dezember verläßt er die Galerie und ist wieder einmal ohne US-Galeristen. Im November wird eine Ausstellung des Œuvres Basquiats in der Kestner-Gesellschaft Hannover eröffnet; sie umfaßt etwa sechzig Arbeiten.

1987 Basquiat hat eine Einzelausstellung von 12 Gemälden in der Galerie Daniel Templon in Paris. Der Tod Andy Warhols am 22. Februar erschüttert Basquiat; trotz der Verschlechterung der Beziehungen zu ihm im vergangenen Jahr wirkt die Nachricht niederschmetternd auf ihn. Er malt einen Grabstein und einige Porträts Warhols, als Erinnerung an den Freund. Im Mai stellt er drei große Arbeiten auf Papier in der Tony Shafrazi Gallery in Soho aus.

1988 Zur Einzelausstellung in der Galerie Yvon Lambert reist Basquiat nach Paris und stellt auch später in der Galerie Hans Mayer in Düsseldorf aus. Für eine Ausstellung in der Vrej Baghoomian Gallery kehrt Basquiat im April nach New York zurück. Basquiat ist schon immer Drogenkonsument gewesen und hat es stets abgelehnt, sich einer Entziehungskur zu unterziehen. Aber bevor er nach Dallas und Los Angeles abreist, um von dort nach Maui zu gehen, sagt er seinem Assistenten, daß er den Drogen für immer ade gesagt habe. Am Freitag, dem 12. August, stirbt er im Haus in der Great Jones Street im Alter von 27 Jahren. Die Autopsie gibt als Todesursache »akute Vergiftung durch diverse Drogen« an. Eine private Beerdigung findet am 17. August in New York in der Frank E. Campbell Funeral Chapel statt. Seine nächsten Anverwandten und besten Freunde sind anwesend, darunter Keith Haring, Francesco Clemente und Paige Paul , um nur einige zu nennen. Jeffery Deitch hält die Gedenkrede. Basquiat wird in Brooklyn begraben. Am 5. November findet eine Trauerfeier für Basquiat in der dortigen Peterskirche statt. Etwa dreihundert Freunde und Bewunderer finden sich ein. Die Musik steuern die Gray-Gruppe und andere bei. Ein Gelegenheitsgedicht des deutschen Künstlers A. R. Penck, »Gedicht für Basquiat«, wird von Suzanne Mallouk, einer früheren Freundin Basquiats, vorgetragen.

Ausstellung: Jean Michel Basquiat, Paintings and Drawings 1980-1988, Gagosian Gallery, Beverly Hills 1998

Einzelausstellungen
One Man Exhibitions

1981

»SAMO«, Galleria d'Arte Emilio Mazzoli, Modena, May 23 – June 20.

1982

Annina Nosei Gallery, New York, March 6 – April 1.

Larry Gagosian Gallery, Los Angeles, April 8 – May 8.

Galerie Bruno Bischofberger, Zurich, September 11 – October 9.

Galleria Mario Diacono, Rome, October 23 – November 20 (brochure).

Fun Gallery, New York, November 4 – December 7.

Galerie Delta, Rotterdam, December (catalogue).

Blum/Helman, New York.

Marlborough Gallery, New York.

1983

Annina Nosei Gallery, New York, February 12 – March 3.

Larry Gagosian Gallery, Los Angeles, March 8 – April 2.

Galerie Bruno Bischofberger, Zurich, September 24 – October 22.

Akira Ikeda Gallery, Tokyo, November 14 – December 10.

Cafe West Beach, Venice.

1984

Mary Boone Gallery, New York, NY, May 5 – 26 (catalogue)

The Fruitmaker Gallery, Edinburgh, Scotland, August 11 – September 23;
Institute of Contemporary Arts, London, December 15, 1984 – January 27, 1985;
Museum Boymans-van Beuningen, Rotterdam, February 9 – March 31, 1985 (catalogue).

Carpenter + Hochman Gallery, Dallas, September 20 – October 20

1985

Galerie Bruno Bischofberger, Zurich, January 19 – February 16 (catalogue).

University Art Museum, University of California, Berkeley, January – March, travelled to La Jolla Museum of Contemporary Art, La Jolla, May 4 – June 16 (brochure).

Mary Boone Gallery, New York, NY, March 2 – March 23 (catalogue).

»Jean Michel Basquiat: Paintings«, Akira Ikeda Gallery, Tokyo, December 2 – 25 (catalogue).

»Jean Michel Basquiat: Paintings from 1982«, Annina Nosei Gallery, New York, December 14, 1985 – January 9, 1986.

1986

Larry Gagosian Gallery, Los Angeles, January 7 – February 11.

Fay Gold Gallery, Atlanta, February 7 – March 5.

Galerie Bruno Bischofberger, Zurich, April 26 – June 30.

Galerie Thaddaeus Ropac, Salzburg, July 27 – August 31 (catalogue).

»Drawings,« Akira Ikeda Gallery, Nagoya, September 8 – 30.

Centre Culturel Francais d'Abidjan, Ivory Coast, October 10 – November 7.

Galerie Delta, Rotterdam, November.

Kestner-Gesellschaft, Hanover, November 28, 1986 – January 25, 1987 (catalogue).

Galerie Michael Werner, Cologne, 1986.

1987

Galerie Daniel Templon, Paris, January 10 – February 7.

Akira Ikeda Gallery, Tokyo, February 7 – 28 (catalogue).

Tony Shafrazi Gallery, New York, May 23 – June 13.

Galerie Thaddaeus Ropac, Salzburg, June 6 – 31.

»Jean Michel Basquiat – Drawings«, P.S. Gallery, Tokyo, October 8 – December 4, (catalogue).

1988

Galerie Yvon Lambert, Paris, January 9 – February 10.

Galerie Beaubourg, Paris, January 9 – February 16.

Galerie Hans Mayer, Dusseldorf, January 12 – March 15.

Galerie Michael Haas, Berlin, February 5 – March 12.

Vrej Baghoomian Gallery, New York, April 29 – June 11.

Galerie Thaddaeus Ropac, Salzburg, June 15 – July 26.

Fay Gold Gallery, Atlanta, September 6 – October 4.

Gallery Schlesinger Limited, New York, November.

Annina Nosei Gallery, New York, December 3, 1988 – January 14, 1989.

1989

Kestner-Gesellschaft, Hanover, Germany, September 28 – October 22 (catalogue).

Vrej Baghoomian Gallery, New York, October 21 – November 25 (catalogue).

Galerie Enrico Navarra, Paris, November 8 – December 31 (catalogue).

Dau al Set, Galeria d'Art, Barcelona, November – December (catalogue).

»Paintings, Drawings«, Galerie Thaddaeus Ropac, Salzburg.

1990

Galerie Le Gall Peyroulet, Paris, January 23 – March 3.

Galerie Fabien Boulakia, Paris, September 27 – November 3 (catalogue).

Robert Miller Gallery, New York, November 6 – December 1 (catalogue).

1991

P.S. Gallery, Tokyo, Japan, March 4 – May 17.

Galerie de Poche, Paris, December 5 – 28.

1992

Vrej Baghoomian Gallery, New York, February 8 – March 7.

Galerie Eric van de Weghe, Brussels, April 9 – May 23 (catalogue).

Musée Cantini, Marseille, July 3 – September 21 (catalogue).

Installation of »Nu-Nile« & »Untitled«, Metropolitan Museum of Art, New York, October 19, 1992.

Whitney Museum of American Art,
New York, October 23, 1992 –
February 14, 1993;
Menil Collection, Houston,
March 11 – May 9, 1993;
Des Moines Art Center, Iowa,
May 22 – August 15, 1993;
Montgomery Museum of Fine Art,
Alabama, November 18,
1993 – January 9, 1994.

1993

Delta Gallery, Rotterdam.

Salon de Mars, Paris, booth of Galerie
Enrico Navarra.

Alpha Cubic Gallery, Tokyo, March
(catalogue).

Galerie Sho Contemporary Art, Tokyo,
May 11 – June 6.

Galerie Bruno Bischhofberger, Zürich,
June 10 – September 11.

Newport Harbor Art Museum, Newport
Beach, July 10 – September 12, 1993.

FAE, Musee d'Art Contemporain,
Pully-Lausanne,
July 10 – November 7, 1993
(catalogue).

Tony Shafrazi Gallery, New York,
November 20, 1993 – January 8, 1994
(catalogue).

»Jean Michel Basquiat: Peinture, dessin,
ecriture«, Musée Galerie de la Seita,
Paris, December 17, 1993 –
February 26, 1994
(catalogue).

1994

Henry Art Gallery, University of
Washington, Seattle,
February 18 – April 6.

Johnson County Community College
Gallery of Art, Overland Park,
September 11 – October 18.

»Jean Michel Basquiat: Works in Black
and White«, Robert Miller Gallery,
New York, November 15, 1994 –
January 7, 1995.

»Jean Michel Basquiat: The Blue Ribbon
Series«, Mount Holyoke College Art
Museum, South Hadley, MA,
September 8 – December 22, 1994;
Wadsworth Atheneum, Hartford,
January – March 1995;
The Andy Warhol Museum, Pittsburg,
April 12 – September 17, 1995;
The Studio Museum in Harlem, New
York, October 15 – December 31,
1995;

Krannert Art Museum and Kinkead
Pavilion, University of Illinois,
Champaign, January 26 – March 24,
1996;
COCA / Museum of Contemporary Art,
Miami, October 10 – December 7,
1996.

1995

»Two Cents: Works on paper by Jean
Michel Basquiat and Poetry by Kevin
Young«, Center Gallery, Miami-Dade
Community College, Wolfson Cam-
pus, October 20, 1995 – January 14,
1996;
Castellani Art Museum,
Niagara University, New York,
February 2 – March 31, 1996;
The University of Memphis, Memphis,
April 19 – June 22, 1996;
University of South Florida Art Museum,
Tampa, July – August 1996;
Otis Gallery of Art and Design, Los
Angeles, September–October, 1996;
Austin Museum of Art, Austin,
November – Januar, 1997.

1996

»Jean Michel Basquiat: Bodies and
Heads«, Robert Miller Gallery,
February 6 – March 9;
Serpentine Gallery, London, March 6 –
April 21. (catalogue)

»Jean Michel Basquiat: Peintures«,
Galerie Enrico Navarra, Paris,
April 2 – June 12.

»Jean Michel Basquiat: Œuvres sur
papier«, Galeries Lucien Durand
-Enrico Navarra, Pairs,
Mai 3 – June 15 (catalogue).

Junta de Andalucia, Málaga,
Mai 16 – July 7 (catalogue).

The Bruce Museum, Greenwich,
August 4 – September 8.

»Jean Michel Basquiat: A Tribute«,
Tony Shafrazi Gallery, New York,
September 21 – November 23.

»Jean Michel Basquiat: 1980 – 1988«,
Quintana Gallery, Coral Gables,
December 17 – February 21, 1997
(catalogue).

1997

Kaohsiung Museum of Fine Arts,
Kaohsiung, January 26 – April 27;

Taiwan Museum of Art, Taiwan,
May 4 – June 4 (catalogue).

»Jean Michel Basquiat Œuvres Sur
Papier«, Fondation Dina-Vierny-Musée
Maillol, Paris,
May 23 – September 29.

Gallery Hyundai, Séoul, July 15 –
August 17 (catalogue).

»King for a Decade – Jean Michel
Basquiat«, Parco Gallery, Tokyo,
July 22 – September 17 (catalogue).

Art Beatus, Vancouver, September 12 –
October 16 (catalogue).

Big Step, Inc. Isaka, October 16 – 21.

Mitsukochi Museum, Tokyo,
October 28 – November 24;
MIMOCA, Marugame, April 18 – May 31,
1998 (catalogue).

»Jean Michel Basquiat: Obras Sobre
Papeis«, Museo Nacional de Bellas
Artes, Buenos Aires, December 8 –
February 13, 1998 (catalogue).

1998

»Jean Michel Basquiat: Paintings and
Drawings 1980 – 1988«, Gagosian
Gallery, Los Angeles, February 12 –
March 14 (catalogue).

»Jean Michel Basquiat: Obras Sobre
Papeis«, Museu de Arte Moderna,
Recife, April 1 – May 31 (catalogue).

Tony Shafrazi Gallery, New York,
April 25 – May 30.

»Jean Michel Basquiat: Pinturas/Obras
Sobre Papeis«, Pinacoteca, Sao Paulo,
June 16 – August 23 (catalogue).

Le tête d'obsédienne, La Seyne-sur-Mer,
June 26 – August 14 (catalogue).

»Jean Michel Basquiat, Témoignage
1977 – 1988«, Galerie Jérôme de
Noirmont, Paris,
October 2 – November 27.

1999

»Jean Michel Basquiat«,
KunstHausWien, Vienna,
February 11 – May 2, 1999 (catalogue)

»Jean Michel Basquiat«, Centre culturel
L'Espal, Le Mans,
April 29 – June 16, 1999 (catalogue)

»Jean Michel Basquiat«, Civico Museo
Revoltella, Trieste,
May 15 – September 15, 1999
(catalogue)

»Basquiat a Venezia«, Fondazione
Bevilacqua La Masa, Venice,
June 9 – October 30, 1999 (catalogue)

»Jean Michel Basquiat, Werke auf Papier / works on paper«, StadtGalerie, Klagenfurt,
June 18 – September 28, 1999 (catalogue)

»Basquiat«, Galleria Dante Vecchiato, Forte dei Marmi (Ort?),
July 10 – August 9, 1999 (catalogue)

»Basquiat«, Galleria Dante Vecchiato, Cortina d' Ampezzo,
August 6 – August 29, 1999 (catalogue)

»Basquiat a Napoli«, Museo Civico Castel Nuovo, Naples,
December 19, 1999 – February 27, 2000 (catalogue)

2000

»Jean Michel Basquiat«, Stephen Lacey Gallery, London,
February 16 – March 18, 2000

»Jean Michel Basquiat«, Galerie Eduard Mitterrano, Genève,
June 8 – July 18, 2000

»Basquiat en la Habana«, Fundación Havana Club, Casa de las Américas, Havana,
Daten fehlen (catalogue)

2001

»Jean Michel Basquiat hits on paper«, PICTUREshow, Berlin,
July 12 – September 23, 2000

Gemeinschafts- ausstellungen
Exhibitions of Collaborations

(Jean Michel Basquiat, Andy Warhol, Francesco Clemente):

1984

Galerie Bruno Bischofberger, Zurich. Collaborations: Jean Michel Basquiat, Francesco Clemente, Andy Warhol, September 15 – October 13. (catalogue).

1985

Akira Ikeda Gallery, Tokyo. Collaborations: Jean Michel Basquiat, Francesco Clemente, Andy Warhol, January 14 – 31. (catalogue).

Tony Shafrazi Gallery, New York. Warhol and Basquiat paintings, September 14 – October 19.

1986

Akira Ikeda Gallery, Tokyo. Collaborations: Jean Michel Basquiat, Andy Warhol, September 8 – 30 (catalogue).

Galerie Bruno Bischofberger, Zurich. Collaborations: Jean Michel Basquiat, Andy Warhol. November 15, 1986 – January 17, 1987 (catalogue).

1988

Mayor Rowan Gallery and David Grob Ltd., London. Collaborations: Andy Warhol, Jean Michel Basquiat. November 21, 1988 – January 21, 1989. (catalogue).

1989

Rooseum, Malmö, Sweden, with Julian Schnabel, April 8 – May 28 (catalogue).

Didier Imbert Fine Arts, Paris. Collaborations: Andy Warhol, Jean Michel Basquiat. September 28 – November 25. (catalogue).

1990

Ho-Am Gallery, Seoul, Korea. Jean Michel Basquiat, Andy Warhol. October 1 – 31

»Keith Haring, Jean Michel Basquiat: Paintings«, Tony Shafrazi Gallery, New York, December 15, 1990 – January 26, 1991.

1991

Sonje Museum Of Contemporary Art, Kyongio, Korea. September 14 – October 20.

The National Museum of Contemporary Art, Seoul. November 1 – 30 Collaboration: Andy Warhol and Jean Michel Basquiat. (catalogue).

1996

Museum Fridericianum, Kassel. February 4 – May 5. Museum Villa Stuck, Munich. July 25 – September 25.

Collaboration: Warhol – Basquiat – Clemente. (catalogue).

Gruppenausstellungen – eine Auswahl
Selected Group Exhibitions

1980

»Times Square Show«, Colab (Collaborative Projects Incorporated) and Fashion Moda (organizers) 41st Street and Seventh Avenue, New York, July

1981

»New York/New Wave«, P.S. 1, Institute for Art and Urban Resources, Long Island City, NY, February 15 – April 5.

»Lower Manhattan Drawing Show«, Mudd Club, New York, NY, February 22 – March 15.

»Beyond Words: Graffiti Based-Rooted-Inspired Works«, Mudd Club, New York, April 9 – 24.

»Public Address«, Annina Nosei Gallery, New York, October 31 – November 19.

»Group Show«, Annina Nosei Gallery, New York, December 19, 1981 – January 24, 1982

1982

»Body Language: Current Issues in Figuration«, University Art Gallery, San Diego State University, CA, March 13 – April 10 (catalogue).

»New New York«, University Fine Arts Galleries, School of Visual Arts, Florida State University, Tallahasse, FL, March 17 – April 17; Metropolitan Museum and Art Centers, Coral Gables, FL, July 9 – August 30 (catalogue).

»Transavanguardia: Italia/America«, Galleria Civica del Comune di Modena, Modena, March 21 – May 2 (catalogue).

»Anaguardia Transavanguardia, 68 to 77«, Mura Aurelane da Porta Metronia a Porta Metronia, Rome, April – July (catalogue).

»New Work«, Sidney Janis Gallery, New York, NY, May 5 – June 3.

»The Pressure to Paint«, Marlborough Gallery, New York, NY, June 4 – July 9 (catalogue).

»Dokumenta 7«, Kassel, June 19 – September 23 (catalogue).

»The Expressionist Image: American Art from Pollock to Today«, Sidney Janis Gallery, New York, October 9 – 30.

»New York Now«, Kestner-Gesellschaft, Hanover, November 26 – January 23, 1983;
Kunstverein München, Munich, February 2 – March 6, 1983;
Musée Cantonal des Beaux-Arts, Lausanne, March 30 – May 15, 1983;
Kunstverein für die Rheinlande und Westfalen, Düsseldorf, July 22 – August 28, 1983. (catalogue)

1983

»Champions«, Tony Shafrazi Gallery, New York, January – February (catalogue).

»1983 Biennial Exhibition«, Whitney Museum of American Art, New York, March 15 – May 29 (catalogue).

»Intoxication«, Monique Knowlton Gallery, New York, April 9 – May 7.

»Back to the USA: Amerikanische Kunst der Siebziger und Achtziger«, Kunstmuseum Luzern, Luzern, Switzerland, May 31–July 31;
Rheinisches Landesmuseum Bonn (organizer), October 27, 1983 – January 15, 1984;
Wurttembergischer Kunstverein, Stuttgart, April – June 1984 (catalogue).

»Group Show«, Annina Nosei Gallery, New York, NY, June 11 – July 29.

»Food for the Soup Kitchen«, Fashion Moda, Bronx, NY, October 1 – 15.

»Mary Boone and Her Artists«, The Seibu Museum of Art, Tokyo, October 6 – 18 (catalogue).

»From the Street«, Greenville County Museum of Art, SC, October 25–November 20.

»Expressive Malerei nach Picasso«, Galerie Beyeler, Basel, October – December (catalogue).

»Written Imagery Unleashed in the Twentieth Century«, Fine Arts Museum of Long Island, Hempstead, NY, November 1983 – January 1984.

»Post-Graffiti«, Sidney Janis Gallery, New York, December 1 – 31.

»Paintings«, Mary Boone Gallery, New York, December 3 – 31.

»Terminal New York«, Brooklyn Navy Yard, New York.

»New York«, Sidney Janis Gallery, New York.

»Selected Works«, Galerie Ulrike Kantor, Los Angeles.

»Contemporary Drawings«, Delahunty Gallery, Dallas.

1984

»Van der Zee Memorial Show: James Van der Zee, 1886 – 1983«, New York City Department of Cultural Affairs, New York, February 1 – March 2.

»Modern Expressionists: German, Italian and American Painters«, Sidney Janis Gallery, New York, NY, March 10 – April 7.

»Since the Harlem Renaissance: 50 Years of Afro-American Art«, Center Gallery of Bucknell University, Lewisburg, PA, April 13 – June 6;
The Amelie A. Wallace Art Gallery, State University of New York, College at Old Westbury, NY, November 1 – December 9;
Munson-Williams-Proctor Institute Museum of Art, Utica, NY, January 11 – March 3, 1985
The Art Gallery, University of Maryland, College Park, MD, March 21 – May 3, 1985;
The Chrysler Museum, Norfolk, VA, July 19 – September 1, 1985;
Museum of Art, Pennsylvania State University, University Park, PA, September 22 – November 1, 1985 (catalogue).

»Arte Di Frontiera: N.Y. Graffiti«, Galleria Communale d'Arte Moderna di Bologna, Bologna, April (catalogue).

»Painting and Sculpture Today«, Indianapolis Museum of Art, May 1 – June 10 (catalogue).

»Via New York«, Musée d'Art Contemporain, Montreal, May 8 – June 24 (catalogue).

»An International Survey of Recent Painting and Sculpture«, The Museum of Modern Art, New York, NY, May 17 – August 19 (catalogue).

»American Neo-Expressionists«, The Aldrich Museum of Contemporary Art, Ridgefield, CT, May 20 – September 9 (catalogue).

»Art«, Area Club, New York, May.

»Drawings by 11 Artists«, Willard Gallery, New York, September 5 – October 6.

»Content: A Contemporary Focus, 1975 – 1984«, Hirshhorn Museum and Sculpture Garden, Smithsonian Institution, Washington, DC, October 4, 1984 – January 6, 1985 (catalogue).

»Painting Now: The Restoration of Painterly Figuration«, Kitakyushu Municipal Museum of Art, Japan, October 6 – 28 (catalogue).

»The East Village Scene«, Institute of Contemporary Art, University of Pennsylvania, Philadelphie, PA, October 12 – December 2 (catalogue).

»Figuration Libre France/USA«, Musée d'Art Moderne de la Ville de Paris, December 21, 1984 – February 17, 1985.

»Aspekte amerikanischer Kunst der Gegenwart«, Neue Galerie-Sammlung Ludwig, Aachen, Germany.

»New Art«, Musée d'Art Contemporain, Montreal.

1985

»XIII Biennale de Paris«, Grand Halle du Parc de la Villette, Paris, March 21 – May 21 (catalogue).

»The Door«, Annina Nosei Gallery, New York, June 7 – July 7 (catalogue).

»Das Oberengadin in der Malerei«, Segantini Museum, St. Moritz, June 20 – October 20.

»Drawing the Line: Painting«, Annina Nosei Gallery, New York, September 21 – October 17.

»Vom Zeichnen: Aspekte der Zeichnung 1960 – 1985«, Frankfurter Kunstverein, Frankfurt, November 19, 1985 – January 1, 1986;
Kasseler Kunstverein, Kassel, January 15 – February 23, 1986;
Museum Moderner Kunst, Vienna, March 13 – April 27, 1986 (catalogue).

»Drawings«, Knight Gallery, Spirity Square Arts Center, Charlotte, NC, December 20, 1985 – February 7, 1986.

»Basquiat and James Surles«, La Jolla Museum of Contemporary Art, La Jolla, CA.

»7000 Eichen«, Kunsthalle, Tübingen; Kunsthalle, Bielefeld

»The Chi-Chi Show«, Massimo Audiello Gallery, New York.

1986

»An American Renaissance: Painting and Sculpture Since 1940«, Fort Lauderdale Museum of Art, Fort Lauderdale, January 12 – March 30.

»Figure as Subject: The Last Decade«, Selections from the Permanent Collection of the Whitney Museum of American Art, Equitable Center, New York, February 13 – June 4 (catalogue).

»75th American Exhibition«, The Art Institute of Chicago, Chicago, March 8 – April 27 (catalogue).

»Contemporary Issues III«, Holman Hall Art Gallery, Trenton State College, NJ, April 2 – 25.

»Portrait of a Collector: Stephane Janssen«, Louisiana Museum of Modern Art, Humblebachk, Denmark, April 5 – May 11;
University Art Museum, California State University, Long Beach, CA, January 27 – March 8, 1987 (catalogue).

»Heads«, Motokoff Gallery, New York, April – May.

»Zeichen, Symbole, Graffiti in der aktuellen Kunst«, Suermondt-Ludwig-Museum und Museumsverein Aachen, Germany, July 6 – August 17 (catalogue).

»Esprit de New York: Paintings and Drawings«, Galerie Barbara Farber, Amsterdam, July 18–24.

»Prospekt 86«, Frankfurter Kunstverein, Frankfurt, September 9 – November 2 (catalogue).

»Focus on the Image: Selections from the Rivendell Collection«, The Art Museum Association of America, San Francisco (organizer);
Phoenix Art Museum, AZ, October 5, 1986 – February 7, 1987;
The University of Oklahoma Museum of Art, Norman, April 25 – August 30, 1987.
Munson-Williams-Proctor Institute Museum of Art, Utica, NY, September 27, 1987 – March 20, 1988;
University of South Florida Art Galleries, Tampa, April 17 – September 10, 1988;
Lakeview Museum of Art and Sciences, Peoria, IL, October 1, 1988 – January 2, 1989;
University Art Museum, California State University, Long Beach, January 30 – May 28, 1989;
Laguna Gloria Art Museum, Austin, TX, June 25, 1989 – January 2, 1990 (catalogue).

»1976–1986: Ten Years of Collecting Contemporary American Art. Selections from the Edward R. Downe, Jr. Collection«, Wellesley College Museum, MA, November 13, 1986 – January 18, 1987 (catalogue).

»New Paintings«, Larry Gagosian Gallery, Los Angeles.

»Basquiat-Combas Peintures, Louis Cane Sculptures«, Galerie Beaubourg, Paris.

1987

»Avant-Garde in the Eighties«, Los Angeles County Museum of Art, April 23 – July 12 (catalogue).

»The East Village Force de Frappe Comes to the South Bronx«, Fashion Moda, Bronx, NY, May 9 – June 1.

»Pop Art from the USA and Europe from the Ludwig Collection«, Forte Belvedere, Florence, July 28 – August 28.

»16@56: Summer Salon«, 56 Bleecker Gallery, New York, July 28 – August 28.

»The Frederick R. Weisman Collection: An International Survey«, San Antonio Art Institute, TX, September 16 – October 16.

»New York Graffiti«, Ludwigshafen, Wilhelm-Hack Museum, September 17 – October 25.

»Logos«, Anne Plumb Gallery, New York, NY, December 19, 1987 – January 23, 1988.

»Works on Paper«, Tony Shafrazi Gallery, New York.

1988

»An Eclectic Eye: Selections from the Frederick R. Weisman Art Foundation«, Bridge Center for Contemporary Art, El Paso, TX, and New Mexico State University, Las Cruces, NM, January 11–December 14;
Cheney Cowles Art Museum, Spokane, WA, January 6 – February 12, 1989;
Boise Art Museum, Idaho, April 15 – June 11, 1989;
University of Wyoming Art Museum, Laramie, June 25 – October 22, 1989;
Virginia Beach Center for the Arts, VA, November 13, 1989 – January 28, 1990;
Gibbes Art Gallery, Charleston, SC, March 9 – May 4, 1990.

»1900 to Now: Modern Art from Rhode Islands Collections«, Museum of Art, Rhode Island School of Design, Providence, RI, January 22 – May 1.

»Figure as Subject: The Revival of Figuration since 1975«, Whitney Museum of American Art at the Equitable Center, New York, February 13 – June 4;
Erwin A. Ulrich Museum of Art, Wichita State University, KS, April 6 – June 12;
The Arkansas Arts Center, Little Rock, AK, June 24 – August 21;
Amarillo Art Center, Texas, September 19 – October 22;
Utah Museum of Fine Arts, University of Utah, Salt Lake City, November 13, 1988 – January 15, 1989;
Madison Art Center, Madison, WI, February 4 – March 26, 1989 (brochure).

»Rebop«, Paula Allen Gallery, New York, April 26 – May 27.

»After Street Art«, Boca Raton Museum of Art, FL, April 29 – May 29.

»Works on Paper«, Gabrielle Bryers Gallery, New York.

»Works on Paper«, Michael Maloney Gallery, Los Angeles.

»L'art Contemporain à la Defense: Les Années 80 Vues par Cinq Galeries«, Galerie La Defense Art 4, Paris

»Art et Langage: Années 80 Œuvres Choisies«, Centre d'Histoire de L'art Contemporain, Quimper (catalogue).

1989

»Modern and Contemporary Master Drawings«, Rosa Esman Gallery, New York, January 6 – 28.

»Words«, Tony Shafrazi Gallery, New York, NY, January 21 – February 18.

»1979–1989: American, Italian, Mexican Art from the collection of Francesco Pellizzi«, Hofstra Museum, Hofstra University, Hempstead, New York, April 16 – May 26, travelled to Lehigh University Art Galleries, Ralph Wilson Gallery, Bethlehem, PA, September 8 – November 2 (catalogue).

»The Chase Manhattan Bank Collection 1974–1989«, Yokohama Museum of Art, Japan, June 18 – October 1.

»A Decade of American Drawing 1980–1989«, Daniel Weinberg Gallery, Los Angeles, July 15 – August 26.

»The Blues Aesthetics: Black Culture and Modernism«, The Washington Project for the Arts, Washington, DC, September 14 – December 9;
California Afro-American Museum, Los Angeles, January 12 – March 4, 1990;

Duke University Museum of Art, Durham, NC, March 23 – May 20, 1990;
Blaffer Gallery, University of Houston, June 8 – July 31, 1990;
The Studio Museum in Harlem, New York, September 16 – December 30, 1990 (catalogue).

»Selected Americans«, Edward Totah Gallery, London, November 28 – December 16, 1988.

1990

»Summer Works on Paper«, Fay Gold Gallery, Atlanta

»Selected Works«, The Greenberg Gallery, St. Louis.

»Section Americaine«, Galerie Hadrien-Thomas, Paris,
January 10 – February 24.

»Par hassard: A Changing Installation of Recent Acquisitions«, Douglas Drake Gallery, Santa Monica, CA,
May 12 – June 10.

»Gesture and Signature«, Michael Kohn Gallery, Santa Monica,
May 12 – June 10.

»The Decade Show: Frameworks of Identity in the 1980's«, Museum of Contemporary Hispanic Art, The New Museum of Contemporary Art and the Studio Museum of Harlem, New York,
May 12 – August 19 (catalogue).

»21 Jahre Internationale Kunstmesse Basel, Art 21'90«, Galerie Hans Mayer, Düsseldorf, at Basel Art Fair,
June 13 – 18.

»Faces«, Marc Richards Gallery, Los Angeles, June 29 – July 28.

»Pharmakon '90«, Nippon Convention Center, International Exhibition Hall, Tokyo, July 28 – August 20 (catalogue).

»The Last Decade: American Artists of the 80's«, Tony Shafrazi Gallery, New York, September 15 – October 27 (catalogue).

»Language in Art«, The Aldrich Museum of Contemporary Art, Ridgefield, CT, October 20, 1990 – January 6, 1991.

»Works on Paper«, Cavaliero Fine Arts, New York, November 2 – December 1.

»Quickdraw: American Master Drawings Since 1959«, Frank Bernaducci Gallery, New York,
November 2 – December 1.

1991

»The 1980's: A Selected View from the Permanent Collection of the Whitney Museum of American Art«, Whitney Museum of American Art, New York, January 16 – March 24.

»Works & #«, Museum of Contemporary Art, Wright State University, Dayton, April 1 – May 18.

»An Aspect of Contemporary Art«, Setagaya Art Museum, Tokyo, April 2 – May 6.

»Selected Works«, Enrico Navarra Gallery, New York, NY. May 6 – June 20.

»Compassion and Protest: Recent Social and Political Art from the Eli Broad Family Foundation Collection«, San Jose Museum, San Jose,
June 1 – August 25 (catalogue).

»Drawing Acquisitions, 1980 – 1991: Selections from the Permanent Collection of the Whitney Museum of American Art«, Whitney Museum of American Art, New York,
June 12 – September 5 (brochure).

»Mito y Magia en America: los Ochenta«, Museo de Arte Contemporaneo de Monterrey, Mexico,
June – September (catalogue).

»Portrait on Paper«, Robert Miller Gallery, New York, June 25–August 2.

»Art of the 1980's: Selections from the Collection of the Eli Broad Family Foundation«, Duke University Museum of Art, Durham, NC, September 20, 1991 – January 5,1992.

»Devil on the Stairs: Looking Back on the Eighties«, Institute of Contemporary Art, University of Pennsylvania, Philadelphia, October 4, 1991 – January 5, 1992;
The Forum and Washington University Gallery of Art, St. Louis, February 1 – March 22, 1992;
Newport Harbor Art Museum, Newport Beach, CA, April 16 – June 21, 1992 (catalogue).

»Domenikos Theotokopoulos: A Dialogue«, Philippe Briet Gallery, New York, December 5, 1991 – January 25, 1992.

»A Passion for Art: Watercolors and Works on Paper«, Tony Shafrazi Gallery, New York, December 7, 1991 – January 25, 1992.

»Works on Paper«, Annina Nosei Gallery, New York, December 10, 1991 – January 7, 1992.

»American Artists of the 80's«, Palazzo delle Albere, Museo Provinciale d'Arte, Trento, Italy,
December 18, 1991 – March 1, 1992 (catalogue).

1992

»Paris Connections: African American Artists in Paris«, Bomani Gallery and Jernigan Wicker Fine Arts, San Francisco, January 14 – February 29 (catalogue).

»Allegories of Modernism: Contemporary Drawing«, The Museum of Modern Art, New York, NY, February 16 – May 5 (catalogue).

»An Exhibition for Satyajit Ray«, Philippe Briet Gallery, New York, April 11 – May 16.

»Passions and Cultures: Selected Works from the Rivendell Collection, 1967 – 1991«, The Richard and Marieluise Black Center for Curatorial Studies, Bard College, Annandale-on-Hudson, NY, April – October (brochure).

»Ars Pro Domo«, Gesellschaft für Moderne Kunst and Museum Ludwig, Cologne, May 22 – August 9.

»The Power of the City/The City of Power«, Whitney Museum of American Art, Downtown Branch, New York, May 20 – July 10 (catalogue).

»Gifts and Acquisitions in Context«, Whitney Museum of American Art, New York, May 22 – September 20.

»Jean Michel Basquiat, Jonathan Borofsky, Richard Bosman, Kang So Lee, Terry Winters«, Haenah-Kent Gallery, New York, June 6 – July 10.

»Baziotes to Basquiat .... and Beyond«, Bellas Artes, Santa Fe, August 20 – September 30.

»X Mostra de Gravura, Curitiba/ Mostra America«, Fundacio Cultural de Curtiaba, October 16 – December 6.

»Dream Singers, Story Tellers: An African American Presence«, Fukui Fine Arts Museum (organized by New Jersey State Museum), November 6 – December 2;
Tokushima Modern Art Museum, January 23 – March 7, 1993;
Otani Memorial Art Museum, April 10 – May 9, 1993;
New Jersey State Museum, Trenton, August 7, 1993 – March 20, 1994.

1993

»1982–83: Ten Years After«,
Tony Shafrazi Gallery, New York,
May 7–July 30.

»Extravagant: The Economy of
Elegance«, Tony Shafrazi Gallery,
New York, January 30 – February 28
(in collaboration with Jonathan
Seliger).
Russisches Kulturzentrum, Berlin,
May 7 – June 27.

»The Theatre of Refusal: Black Art and
Mainstream Criticism«, Fine Arts
University of California, Irvine,
April 8 – May 12.

1994

»The Hamon and Harriet Kelley
Collection of African American Art«,
San Antonio Museum of Art, Texas,
February 4 – April 3 (catalogue).

»The Shaman as Artist / The Artist as
Shaman«, Aspen Art Museum,
Aspen, February 10 – April 10
(catalogue).

»Art in the Present Tense: The Aldrich´s
Curatorial History, 1964 – 1994«,
Aldrich Museum, Ridgefield,
May 15 – September 18.

»Against all odds: The Healing Powers of
Art«, Ueno Royal Museum, Tokyo;
Hakone Open Air Museum,
Kanagaura-ken.

»Maîtres Modernes et Contempor-
ains«,Exposition inaugurale, Galerie
Jérôme de Noirmont, Paris,
October 6 – December 6 (catalogue).

1995

»A New York Time: Drawings of the
Eighties«, The Bruce Museum,
Greenwich, January 22 – April 23
(catalogue).

»Passions Privées«, Musée d'Art Moderne de la Ville de Paris, Paris, December 19 – March 24, 1996 (catalogue).

1996

»Comme un oiseau«, Fondation Cartier
pour l'Art Contemporain, Paris,
June 19 – October 13 (catalogue).

»Thinking Print: Books to Billboards
1980 – 1995«, Museum of Modern
Art, New York,
June 20 – September 10.

»Nouvelles Impressions d'Afrique«,
Galerie Beaubourg, Vence,
July 8 – November 30 (catalogue).

»Bill Traylor, Philip Guston, Jean Michel
Basquiat, Gary Romarin«, John
McEnroe Gallery, New York,
September 13 – October 26
(catalogue).

1997

»35 Jaar: 1962 – 1997«, Delta Gallery,
Rotterdam, January 8 – February 8.

»35 Jaar Delta Werken«, Delta Gallery,
Rotterdam, March 15 – June 15.

»In Your Face: Keith Haring, Jean Michel
Basquiat, Kenny Scharf«, Malca Fine
Art, New York, June 17 – August 30
(catalogue).

1998

»Au Fil du Trait – De Matisse à Basquiat«, Carré d'Art, Nîmes,
June 26 – September 27 (catalogue).

»L'intraçable frontière«, Espace EDF-
Bazacle, Toulouse, July 3 – 19
(catalogue).

»Portraits Obscured«, Gagosian Gallery,
New York, July 20 – September 12.

1999

»Pittura Dura, Dal Graffitlamo alla Street
Art«, Palazzo Bricherasio, Turin,
November 24, 1999 – January 30,
2000 (catalogue)

»Portrait Collection of Mr. Chow«, galerie
Enrico Navarra, Paris,
December 1, 1999 – January 10, 2000
(catalogue)

2000

»Haiti, Anges et Démons«, Halle
Saint-Pierre, Paris,
March 20 – June 30, 2000 (catalogue)

2001

»Tribù dell'arte«, Galleria communale
d'arte moderna e contemporanea,
Rome,
April 21 – June 23, 2001

Ausgewählte Literatur
Bücher und Kataloge

Selected Bibliography
Books and Catalogues

Jean Michel Basquiat Paintings 1981-
1984 (catalogue), The Fruitmarket
Gallery, Edinburgh.
Text: Marl Francis

Jean Michel Basquiat Drawings, Edition
Bruno Bischofberger, Zurich, Mary
Boone, New York, 1985.

The Door (catalogue), Annina Nosei
Gallery, New York, 1985.

Jean Michel Basquiat (catalogue), Edition
Bruno Bischofberger, Zurich, 1985.

Collaboration: Jean Michel Basquiat/
Andy Warhol (catalogue), Akira Ikeda
Gallery, Tokyo, 1986.

Jean Michel Basquiat Bilder (paintings)
1984-1986 (catalogue), Galerie
Thaddaeus Ropac, Salzburg, 1986.

Jean Michel Basquiat New Works
(catalogue), Akira Ikeda Gallery,
Tokyo, 1987.

Michel Enrici, Jean Michel Basquiat,
Editions de la Difference (series
Classique du XXième siècle),
Paris 1989.

Jean Michel Basquiat, Das zeichnerische
Werk (Drawings) (catalogue), Kestner-
Gesellschaft, Hanover, 1989.

Jean Michel Basquiat, Peintures, Sculptures, Oeuvre sur Papier, Dessin
(catalogue - paintings, sculpture,
works on paper, drawings).
Galerie Enrico Navarra, Paris 1989.
Text: Demosthenes Dawetas

Jean Michel Basquiat (catalogue), Vrej
Baghoomian, Inc. New York, 1989.
Text: Francesco Pellizzi, Glenn
O'Brien.

Jean Michel Basquiat (catalogue), Galeria
d'Art Dau Al Set. Barcelona, 1989.

Warhol Basquiat Collaboration
(catalogue), Didier Imbert Fine Art,
Paris 1989.
Text: Grégoire Müller.

Basquiat, (catalogue), Galerie Boulakia,
Paris 1990.
Text: Nicolas Bourriaud, Henry Geld-
zahler, Remo Guidieri, Sylvie
Philippon, Philippe Piguet, Jano
Rankin Reid, Greg Tate.

Robert Storr, Jean Michel Basquiat
Drawings (catalogue), Robert Miller
Gallery, New York, 1990.

Basquiat Drawings, Preface Robert Storr, Bulfinch Press Book, 1990.

Kyochi Tsuzuki, Jean Michel Basquiat, Art Random Published by Kyoto Shoin International Co., Ltd., Kyoto, Japan, 1992.

Jean Michel Basquiat, A Retrospective (catalogue), Musée Cantini, Marseille, 1992

Jean Michel Basquiat (catalogue), Delta Gallery, Rotterdam, 1992.

Jean Michel Basquiat, The Notebooks, Art and Knowledge, New York, 1993

Maya Angelou, Life doesn't Frighten Me. Poem by Maya Angelou, paintings by Jean Michel Basquiat, published by Stewart, Tabori, Chang, New York, 1993.

Jean Michel Basquiat (catalogue) Whitney Museum of American Art, New York, 1993.
Text: Richard Marshall, David A. Ross, Robert Farris Thompson, René Richard, Klaus Kertess, Greg Tate, Dick Hebdige.

Jean Michel Basquiat, Paintings and Drawings (catalogue), Galerie Sho, Tokyo, 1993.

Jean Michel Basquiat (catalogue), FAE Musée d'Art Contemporain, Pully-Lausanne, 1993.

Two Cents, Works on Paper by Jean Michel Basquiat, Poetry by Kevin Young (catalogue), Centre Gallery, Miami, Castellani Art Museum, Niagra Museum, N.Y., Otis Gallery, Otis College of Arts and Design, California, 1996.

Jean Michel Basquiat, Works on Paper (catalogue), Galeries Lucien Durand-Enrico Navarra, Paris, 1996.

Jean Michel Basquiat (catalogue), Serpentine Gallery, London, 1996.

Jean Michel Basquiat, Two Volumes, published by Galerie Enrico Navarra, Paris, 1996.
Text: Richard Marshall, Jean-Louis Prat.

Jean Michel Basquiat Portraits, 45 Plates, published by Bruno Bischofberger, Zurich, circa 1996-97.
Text: Francesco Clemente

Jean Michel Basquiat, Works on Paper (catalogue), Museo Nacional PE Bellas Artes, Buenos Aires, 1997.

King for a Decade, Jean Michel Basquiat, Korinsha Press Co. Ltd., Tokyo, 1997.

Jean Michel Basquiat, 1980-1988, Paintings, Drawings and Objects (catalogue), Quintana Gallery, Coral Gables, Florida, 1996.

Jean Michel Basquiat, Works on Paper (catalogue), Fondation Dina Vierny, Musée Maillol, Paris, 1997.

Jean Michel Basquiat, Paintings and Drawings 1980–1988, Gagosian Gallery, Los Angeles, 1998.

Phoebe Hoban, Basquiat, A Quick Killing in Art, a biography published by Viking Press, N.Y., 1998.

Jean Michel Basquiat, Témoignage 1977-1988 (catalogue), Galerie Jérôme de Noirmont, Paris 1998.

Videos und Filme
Videos and Films

1983

Tshinkel, Paul, »Young Expressionists«: Jean-Michel Basquiat at the Fun Gallery, Francesco Clemente at the Mary Boone Gallery and Sperone Westwater Gallery, Julian Schnabel at the Leo Castelli Gallery. Art/New York, a video magazine on art, No.: 19.

1989

Jean-Michel Basquiat (1960-1988), Art/New York, a video magazine on art, No.: 30.

1990

Dunlopp, Geoff, Jean-Michel Basquiat: »Shooting Star«, London, England, Illuminations TV.

1993

»Jean-Michel Basquiat, Artists Achievements Debated«, Sunday morning, January 24, CBS Television, 8 mm.

1997

»Basquiat«, a feature film by Julian Schnabel, Miramax Films and Jon Kilik present a Peter Brant, Joseph Allen production.

2001

»Downtown 81«, Originally titled »New York Beat«, Director: Edo Bertoglio, Screenplay: Glenn O'Brien, Produced by Maripol Fauque